Rebel Private:
Front and Rear

Rebel Private:
Front and Rear

Memoirs of a
Confederate Soldier

━┿ *by* ┿━

William A. Fletcher

Introduction by Richard Wheeler
Afterword by Vallie Fletcher Taylor

A DUTTON BOOK

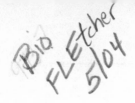

DUTTON
Published by the Penguin Group
Penguin Books USA Inc., 375 Hudson Street,
New York, New York 10014, U.S.A.
Penguin Books Ltd, 27 Wrights Lane,
London W8 5TZ, England
Penguin Books Australia Ltd, Ringwood,
Victoria, Australia
Penguin Books Canada Ltd, 10 Alcorn Avenue,
Toronto, Ontario, Canada M4V 3B2
Penguin Books (N.Z.) Ltd, 182–190 Wairau Road,
Auckland 10, New Zealand

Penguin Books Ltd, Registered Offices:
Harmondsworth, Middlesex, England

First published by Dutton, an imprint of Dutton Signet,
a division of Penguin Books USA Inc.
Distributed in Canada by McClelland & Stewart Inc.

First Printing, July, 1995
10 9 8 7 6 5 4 3 2 1

Copyright © Vallie Fletcher Taylor, 1995
Introduction copyright © Richard Wheeler, 1995
All rights reserved

REGISTERED TRADEMARK—MARCA REGISTRADA

LIBRARY OF CONGRESS CATALOGING-IN-PUBLICATION DATA
Fletcher, W. A. (William Andrew), b. 1839.
Rebel private, front and rear : memoirs of a Confederate soldier /
by William A. Fletcher ; introduction by Richard Wheeler ; afterword
by Vallie Fletcher Taylor.
p.   cm.
Originally published: Beaumont : Press of the Greer print, 1908.
ISBN 0-525-93992-X
1. Fletcher, W. A. (William Andrew), b. 1839.   2. United States—
History—Civil War, 1861–1865—Personal narratives, Confederate.
3. Confederate States of America. Army. Texas Infantry Regiment,
5th—Biography.   4. Soldiers—Texas—Biography.   I. Title.
E605.F58   1995
973.7'82—dc20   94-45324
[B]   CIP

Printed in the United States of America
Set in Cochin and Adobe Garamond
Designed by Julian Hamer

This new edition of Rebel Private: Front and Rear *is dedicated with love and gratitude to the memory of my teachers Vallie Fletcher and William Andrew II, the daughter and grandson of the "Rebel private," and to my children, Vallie Sheryl, Autumn Suzanne, Jordan Ross, and Keith Andrew, and their children. May all of you creatively anticipate tomorrow as you learn to appreciate yesterday.*

—Vallie Fletcher Taylor

CONTENTS

ACKNOWLEDGMENTS

I would like to thank the many people who helped make this new edition of *Rebel Private: Front and Rear* possible: Thanks for the contributions of these historians and archivists: Charlsie Berly, a beautiful lady in her nineties who well remembers Bill Fletcher; W. T. Block, prolific researcher and writer of East Texas history; Jonathan Gerland, archivist of the Sam Houston Regional Library and Research Center in Liberty, Texas; Mel Johnson, researcher of the Texas Forestry Museum in Lufkin, Texas; and David Montgomery and Linda Smith of the Tyrell Historical Library in Beaumont, Texas. Also, thanks to Estelle Perrault of St. Landry Parish, Louisiana; Robert J. Robertson of the Texas Gulf Historical Society; and these friends who gave loving assistance: Paulette Dominiak, Nona Poor, and Trish Kunz.

INTRODUCTION

_{╍═╍}

by Richard Wheeler

There is presently a great deal of public interest in our nation's Civil War, and bookstores are replete with offerings on the topic. Along with works by today's historians are reissues of volumes that appeared during the decades immediately following the war. Included with the latter are numerous memoirs by military participants. Unfortunately, the bulk of these books were written by men of advanced rank, the chief considerations of whom were strategy and tactics and self-justification.

Good memoirs by enlisted men, who saw the war largely in human terms (the angle of strongest appeal to the average reader), are all too few. This lack is gravest on the Southern side, mainly because the Southern army was smaller than that of the North and hence produced fewer chroniclers.

One of the best writers in this limited Southern group is William A. "Bill" Fletcher. But his *Rebel Private: Front and Rear*, which saw first light as a self-published volume in 1908, has remained little known outside the realm of Civil War scholarship. Only with the present edition is the work being offered to a general audience. This is a measure long overdue.

Bill Fletcher's role in the war was of the broadest nature. He served as a foot soldier with Hood's Texans, and as a horseman with Terry's Texas Rangers. His hours of close combat were many. He participated in the early battles around Richmond, was at Second Manassas, Fredericksburg, Gettysburg, and Chickamauga. He assisted with the harassment of Sherman's rear guard during the general's Great March. Two serious wounds were the private's lot along the way. Equally as notable as his combat experiences were his adventures behind the lines.

Bill Fletcher was, all in all, a remarkable person. The product of a frontier environment (western Louisiana and eastern Texas), he was intelligent, resourceful, and long on common sense. His formal education was scant, but he overcame this lack through a devotion to reading. Objective in his view of the human condition, he wasn't afraid to question conventional attitudes. Though poor when he went to war, and handicapped by the economic uncertainties of Reconstruction when he came home, he managed, through innovative lumbering ventures, to die a man of wealth and high social standing.

Living to the age of seventy-five, Fletcher was in his sixties when he composed his book. He wrote entirely from memory, and he paid little attention to the war's strategic and tactical details. These, he knew, could be found in many other places, and they were not important to the story he wanted to tell.

His viewpoint was strictly personal. He concentrated on what he himself had seen and done, and his attention to detail in this respect is superb. His style is lively and frequently amusing, and he is gifted at seizing and holding the reader's interest. Sometimes, in his down-to-earth way, he is sagely philosophical.

The honesty of his narrative is striking. As he paints his colorful word pictures, one senses that the color is based strictly on reality. He makes no attempt to romanticize the war or his part in it. Though his devotion to duty was unfailing, this is not portrayed as a shining virtue but simply as a debt he owed the Southern cause.

There is little in the book about the fanfare of war, about such things as resounding bands and rippling flags. Fletcher prefers to show the reader that campaigning, even aside from combat, is heavy with discomfort and deprivation. He tells of rations becoming scarce, of the campfire's warmth giving way to chills induced by soaking rain, of contagious illnesses. Cleanliness is revealed to be illusive. Uniforms are sometimes worn for days without removal, and there are odious encounters with body lice.

Like all Civil War soldiers, Fletcher knew his share of meetings with civilian females, but little he says about those he met, most of whom were Southerners, suggests romance. Mainly, these women were either helpful or unhelpful to the army's efforts. The reader is left looking in vain for beautiful creatures waving handkerchiefs as the troops marched by.

At the front, Fletcher admits, he and his comrades were frequently unsuccessful with their efforts. They were as apt to fire their weapons without effect as they were to do damage. When Fletcher discusses the Yankees and their abilities, he does so with a fair tongue. He did not subscribe to the notion that Southern fighting spirit would decide the conflict. He believed that the Union, with its superior resources, must be the final victor.

Fletcher's comments about slaughter are not for the

squeamish. He felt not a whit of regret at the sight of the enemy's dead. On the contrary, such scenes elated him. The more blue-coated corpses he saw, the greater his satisfaction. He shrugs at seeming callous in this respect, for his pleasure had a practical foundation: the heavier the enemy's losses, the better his own chances of staying alive. This is a line of thought common to combat soldiers, but few tend to voice it so coolly.

Fletcher narrates his personal exploits so matter-of-factly that the reader must dip deeply into the book before the realization comes that the private was an outstanding soldier.

Though he wasn't immune to fear, he was always able to master it. (Alcohol, he discovered, did not help, was no "fear tonic.") He excelled at the difficult and dangerous business of scouting, and was given many important assignments in this area. Because of his resourcefulness, his comrades looked to him for leadership in tight situations. A proficient forager, he was seldom long without food.

When wounded, he reacted with a steadfast determination to recover and return to duty. (Once badly shot in the foot, he refused amputation and brought the member back to full use.) Captured by the enemy, he promptly began plotting his escape, and, as might be expected, he was clever enough to succeed in this.

Why did so fine a soldier spend the entire war without a commission? Because he chose to turn down his opportunities to attain one. He preferred being an enlisted man, feeling this was the rank that offered him the greatest independence of action, was best suited to his talents.

Fletcher kept his level-headed attitude toward the war to its end, and he had no trouble "sliding back into the Union," as he termed it. He held no grudges, making friends with the

Yankee occupational troops sent to his town, even drinking with them. He found them to be "nice jovial young fellows." Moreover, they were well supplied with money, and they always paid for the drinks. Criticized by his townsmen for this fraternization, Fletcher simply pointed out that the war was over.

The war was over, but it would never be forgotten. And, thanks to writers like Bill Fletcher, its realities would survive through the years. It would be kept from slipping (as often happens with historical events) too deeply into the realm of romance.

Rebel Private: Front and Rear is a valuable book. And now that it has been rescued from near oblivion for presentation to a general readership, there is every reason to believe it will maintain a prominent place in Civil War literature.

Experiences and Observations from the Early Fifties and Through the Civil War

⊹≕⊹

THIS EFFORT is made through memory, as I have no written data, therefore, will not attempt to give names or dates, only in a few instances.

I was born in St. Landry Parish, Louisiana, in 1839. When I was about fourteen years of age I began to notice through listening to the talking of the older people, the trend of feeling in regard to slavery, between the North and South, and as my father* was a close reader and kept fairly well posted on the live topics of the day, and as he had been a slave driver or overseer in Texas at an early date, later on in Louisiana, he was up on the goods and abuses of the system as practised, for he had the advantage while in Texas of having charge of fifteen "likely bucks," as he called them, who were just from their nativity, and who he ran to Louisiana from the Brazos†

---

* Bill's parents were Thomas Fletcher, born in Greenville County, North Carolina, Feb. 18, 1807, and Eliza Miller, born near Murfreesboro, Tennessee, April 9, 1815.
† During the Texas revolution, General Antonio Lopez de Santa Anna, the Mexican dictator, invaded Texas in February 1836. His army marched

1

River when General Santa Anna was invading Texas; and his opinion was that the abuses by inhuman owners were such that an enlightened and humane people would sooner or later abolish it by some method; and he was fearful it would be war, as both North and South seemed to be swayed by the demagog, and it was evident the statesmen were largely in the minority, so if things did not take a different course soon, the blood of the bone and sinew of the government would soon be flowing on a number of hard fought battle fields.

Father's opinion was an unpopular one and as time passed, it got more so and he would rarely express it to but few of his closest friends, who give one the same privilege of expression that they take on subjects of great concern. The hotheaded politician and preacher seemed to be molding public opinion without any regard for the country as a whole. Both North and South were proving, from their view point the justness of their position by both the Bible and Constitution, and from the preacher's views, the Lord was with us for he could prove it by the Bible; while the politician would quote some of the wording of the Constitution, and say: "God and all civilized nations are with us." So with this character of education there was being reared a generation of warriors, and so it was blood—nothing else but blood and we surely spilled it.

---

across Texas in a northeasterly direction with the object of taking possession of the Texas ports and seacoast. The Mexican forces crossed the Brazos River, near present-day Richmond, on April 11, 1836. Thomas Fletcher learned of the invasion when he and the slaves he had purchased ran into the small army of panic-stricken citizens who had abandoned their homes and belongings and were heading east toward the Louisiana border. This group of fleeing citizens is referred to as "The Runaway Scrape" in Texas history.

Father thought a densely settled negro district would be a poor place to have a family during the war, which he said was sure to come; so he sold out and moved to Texas, and settled at Wiess Bluff,* Jasper County, June, 1856. At Wiess Bluff, father found in old man Simon Wiess a well read and intelligent man, and one who reasoned the future as he did; but his moving ideas were somewhat different, as I have heard him remark to father that if he could sell out at not too great a loss he would move to the Republic of Mexico in order to keep his boys out of war. While at Wiess Bluff, about the only mention of war I would hear was by father and Wiess.

Father moved to Beaumont in '59,† and there was not much war agitation heard, but what there was, was very extreme, such as: "I can arm my few negroes and run a whole company of Yanks out of the State," and "one Southerner with his superior marksmanship could shoot down the D——Bluebellies as fast as they would come in sight." In fact, I have often heard the remark before the war and around our camp fires in the early part of the service, that "we would only have a breakfast spell and all those who enlisted first would see the fun." So the impression I received through public clamor had dethroned what little reason I had, as I believed the most that the politician said, and all the preacher said, because he proved it by the Bible; and such ideas as

* Wiess Bluff was in the extreme southwestern portion of Jasper County, Texas, on the east bank of the Neches River. Simon Wiess, a Polish immigrant and merchant, established this river port settlement in 1840.
† The Beaumont of 1859 had grown out of the site of a trading post on the Neches River established by early French and Spanish fur trappers and explorers. The first permanent settlers were Noah and Nancy Tevis, who received a Mexican land grant in 1825. It was then called Tevis Bluff or River Neches Settlement. In 1835, Tevis sold fifty acres of his land to a holding company that laid out the first town site called Beaumont.

father had were then looked upon as the young now feel toward the old—that they may be good, but don't fit the age.

I was on the roof of a two story house putting on the finishing course of shingles when Captain Wm. Rogers* came by and reported war declared and the fall of Fort Sumter. The news was brought from Sabine Pass by an up-river steamer that had just landed, and it made me very nervous thinking the delay of completing the roof might cause me to miss a chance to enlist, so I worked and talked and soon had the roof finished, and made an agreement with Rogers that I would take the train the next day for Houston, and Galveston if necessary, and find some way of enlisting, he paying one-half the expense, which he did. So I boarded a flat car at the appointed time, and in the course of several hours made Liberty; from there I pumped my way to Houston on a hand car.† When I arrived there, which was near night, I started to inquire about the chances to enlist. I soon found there was no effort being made to organize, but that there would be soon; though from appearance and expression there would be no chance for me, as nearly all were going to enlist the first opportunity. The next day I went to Galveston, found conditions about the same as at Houston, so I boarded the first steam boat out for Liberty. When I reached there, I learned that there was a man by the name of O'Brien‡ getting up a

---

* William Rogers was a successful Houston attorney.

† Ron Olson, a Southern Pacific project designer in Austin, and Harold Eason, of the S.P. Engineering Department in Denver, consulted old railroad maps and concluded that in 1861 this would have been a distance of forty miles from station to station.

‡ George W. O'Brien was an attorney and an early settler in Beaumont. At one time he carried mail from Morgan City, Louisiana, through Beaumont to Galveston on horseback. During the first year of the war, a person with means often organized a unit and financed its first operations.

company; so I walked a short distance to his residence in the country. I found that he preferred his home boys, if a sufficient number would enlist. However, with a little persuasion, I got Rogers and I enrolled. I returned home for a few days, then went to Lynchburg and was sworn in. We remained there for some time before starting for Richmond, Virginia. Rogers had accepted a position on a steam boat and was not sworn in. On our way to Richmond we passed through Beaumont and the company received several additional members, and a few joined as we passed through Louisiana.

The parting words of father were: "William, I have long years since seen this had to come and it is a foolish undertaking, as there is no earthly show for Southern success, as our ports will be blocked and the North will not only have advantage of men and means, but the world to draw from, and if you live to return, you will see my predictions are right. While I have opposed it, but as it is here, I will say that you are doing the only honorable thing and that is defending your country."

So from Beaumont we boarded a steam boat for Niblets Bluff, Louisiana. We were hardly out of sight of town before there were gambling groups on different parts of the boat, in full blast. It seemed the boys had thrown off all home restraint in that particular. We reached Niblets Bluff in due time and remained there a few days. While there I met an acquaintance who was running a small store and he proposed a game with me. I accepted, and as he was not bothered with customers, we straddled the counter and played two or three hours at five cents anty. At the finish he was five cents the winner. He then proposed the best two out of three "seven up" for a bottle of lemon syrup and sugar to sweeten, which cost forty cents. I accepted and was the winner. He shut up shop and we went some distance to a spring and made and drank our full of lemonade. That was my first and last game of cards for money.

Leaving Niblets Bluff, we reached New Orleans by marching, boating and railroad transportation. We were quartered in a cotton yard and had but little restriction. The first night there were quite a lot of the boys who went into the city. The next day they gave their experiences, which they claimed were very enjoyable, so the next night there was quite a number of them that wanted to go again, and without much persuasion I joined three of them and boarded a hack and spent a part of the night out. I had twenty odd dollars in gold that was intended for necessities, from time to time, during enlistment and the most of the boys had made similar provisions. I found, however, that I was with a "busted" crowd, for when the hackman wanted fare I paid. Every place we went was "Free Admission," but before we got out, I paid. This was repeated until I was busted, so after having had what we called a "good time" we took a cab and returned to our quarters. When the hack driver called for pay we turned our empty pockets and reported busted, and I have often thought if our acts were what started cabmen collecting in advance.

We boarded box cars at New Orleans and started for Richmond, making slow time. Our rations ran out before we reached Lynchburg, Virginia, and we got awfully hungry, but had no money to buy. When we reached Lynchburg, we stopped a few hours to draw rations, but as soon as we alighted at the depot we found a hogshead of sugar and saw nearby an apple orchard, and before rations were distributed we had about filled up on stewed apples.

When we arrived at Richmond, we marched to camp

about five miles out and remained there some time drilling and forming into regiments, brigades, etc. My company was "F," 5th Texas Infantry, and the brigade was organized with the 1st, 4th and 5th Texas and 3rd Arkansas. In this camp we suffered a good deal with sickness—the most fatal I guess was measles. I had an attack of measles and was sent to the hospital in Richmond and remained there a few days and got tired of hospital life, so I tried to be a good boy and please the woman who had charge of the ward in which I was. I soon persuaded her to get me a discharge, and I returned to camp one cold, frosty morning; the next day I was hauled back a very sick man; was put in a small room that had a coal grate and was instructed to stay in bed and keep well covered up. I lay there a few days with a burning fever, taking such medicine as was prescribed. I had learned the "itch" was getting to be a common complaint in the hospital, and after the fever had somewhat abated, I found I had it, so when the doctor made his next visit I drew my arms from under the covers and showed him the whelps or long red marks of itch, and he said he would send me some medicine that would soon cure it. So I lay covered and rubbed all parts that itched, with medicine, and I guess I got better, or at least thought so, and so reported to the doctor on his next visit. He gave me a lecture on the importance of keeping well covered. That evening I was visited by Jeff Chaison* of "F," and I told him about having the itch. Jeff said: "Bill you have not got any itch, and I bet it is body lice you have, as the house is stacked with them." His remarks made me angry and I talked rather harsh to him for thinking that I was that kind of a filthy being and that I had not as yet ever seen one. As he went

* Jeff Chaison was a well-known early settler of Beaumont.

out he said, "You will when they get grown, as they are as big as a grain of wheat." He had not been gone long and I was yet feeling mean towards Jeff—my finger nails were long and I was scratching and got something under one of them. I drew my hand out from under cover and held it to the light, and there, sure enough, was something alive, for I could see its legs working. I was on my feet instantly and at the window sill, with a full-grown louse crawling before my eyes—such a feeling of disgrace one rarely has. I made an examination of clothing and bedding and saw that I was well supplied with them of all sizes and nits by the hundreds. There was a good fire in the grate and scuttle of coal nearby, so I kept a fire while I held my clothing and bed covering to the heat and cooked the life out of the most of them. My clothing and bedding was well scorched when I got through, but the nits in the seams seemed to be but little changed. That night I slept but little and there was no further notice of doctor's instructions as I was well, less the lice. The next morning I rolled up my lousy clothes and went to the hospital laundry. It seemed to be run exclusively by women and this did not help my predicament any, as I hated to turn my clothing in even to men. I soon saw who was boss, and I went to her and said in a down cast tone, so none of the others could hear me, that my clothing was lousy and I wished she would have them boiled. She spoke in a loud tone, and they all heard and laughed: "Law, child, boiling won't kill them."

I got out of there quickly, feeling thoroughly disgraced and thought if I had the money, cold as it was, I would go into the city and buy clothing, and burn what I had. But as time passed, I got over my feeling of disgrace and learned that all were subjects, under like conditions. I got transferred from the back room I was occupying to a front, on the third floor. On the ground floor under my room there was a fruit merchant and he had a stand that was under my window, on the sidewalk, and one could look down and feast the eye on nice ripe fruit, and this would cause a longing for some. There was one of "F" boys who was an inmate at that time in the hospital—his name was Pemberton, but was nicknamed "Wild Bill." He was a West Texas product and a fine, noble young fellow, and was well up on cowboy lore, therefore originated his nickname. Bill called at my room and while there discovered the fruit. He said that it made him hungry and asked me if I was not hungry for some. I said, "Yes, and I wish that the fellow would keep it inside, or I had some money." He said, "If you will let me operate from your room we will have all the fruit we want, or he will have to move it out of sight, and I do not think there would be any more harm in taking it than the man is doing by tempting a busted fellow." I agreed, and asked how he was going to do it. He said: "Wait and you will see when I come back tomorrow." When Bill returned he had a large fishhook, straightened, and line of suitable length, and with suitable weight where the line was attached to the hook. It made a good harpoon when dropped a few feet. The fruit stand was against the wall and nearly out of sight of the attendant inside. Bill, for a time, was a welcome daily visitor and could be seen about 10 A.M. at my window "fishing," as he called it, for fruit. He operated in this way: Lowered his hook to a point a few feet above the fruit; dropped it, then he would pull it up and repeat. His time of operation was when a customer entered the room. This operation was repeated several days before the stand was kept off of the sidewalk, but Bill and I sure had all the fruit we could eat, until the fellow caught on. We did not think that he ever saw or missed the fruit, but was told by some one. It was sure funny to see his neighbors on the opposite side of the street enjoy the fun. I think some of them looked forward with pleasure and would have others posted, as day by day the sight-seers on the opposite side increased. One Sunday evening a few days after the fruit had been housed, Wild Bill asked me if I was not fruit hungry. My reply was, "Yes." He said: "Let's go and get some, then." I asked: "How?" He said: "Let's go and get our haversacks and go out in town and when we come to a fruit or candy fellow that looks like he has got more than the law allows and is using the sidewalk to keep some of his stuff on, you go inside and make out like you have money and want to buy; let your wants be where the fellow will have to turn his back to the street to get same; or it will be better if he has to climb up. Play him as long as you think is right, for you know there is no harm in looking at what a fellow has to sell; and he cannot think hard of you if the article is not the grade you are after, or the price is too high, and while you are inside, diverting the boss, I will be out running our business." My reply was: "I catch." We were soon on the streets, passing from one stand to the other that only had one attendant. One haversack was soon well supplied and exchange made for an empty one and it was not long before the second one had ample inner contents for convenient carrying. Pard said he could not see any harm in getting stuff in this way, for the fellow never missed it and when one couldn't miss anything, how did he know that he ever had it. He asked me if I had ever before been on an outing like that, and my reply was "No." He said that was the way with lots of fellows. "They could be something if they would try," and if it hadn't been for him I might have been killed before I found out I was good for something;

for I sure was a success on a foraging trip. "Foraging" was the word applied for such outings during the war—in civil life it is called "shoplifting."

As soon as I was about recovered from the measles I took the mumps, and with a lot of others was put on a canal boat and taken some distance to a place, which, if I remember correctly, was called "Huguenot Springs." I remained there until I was able to report for duty. While at the "Springs" I would roam the country some, though I was taking chances in the cold. While out one day and up a well iced persimmon tree, I slipped and was hurt considerably; returned to hospital and was confined to bed several days. I was one in a room of several occupants, and while there we received a visit daily from a nice old maid. She always had something good to eat to divide up with us, and as she was most gabby with me, the boys got to calling her my old girl, and said she showed partiality in her "hand-outs," so when I was confined to bed from the mishap, she was curious to know what was my trouble, and at each visit she became more persistent and I had dodged answering to the limit of my ability, but on entering the room one day she said I sure had to tell her tomorrow what was the matter or she would not give me anything to eat. When she left the boys had their fun at my expense. The next morning the boys started joking again, and asked me what I was going to do and I said: "Wait and see." So at about the usual time "my girl" as the boys called her, made her appearance, looking as sweet and prim as usual, with a plate well piled with "goodies." She was as persistent as ever, and I finally said: "If you must know, I will tell you." The boys commenced laughing. She was soon out of the room, slamming the door, with all the tempting food on the platter. The boys laughed and swore to their heart's content, as they knew all future visits would be only by the hospital attendants.

When I was discharged from the hospital I reported to command near Dunfrees. The Federals and Confederates were camped on opposite sides of the Potomac River. We moved camp in the early part of '62—the men were well equipped with clothing and bedding and nearly all started with an overload, and the roadside during the first day's march was strewn for miles with clothing, blankets, etc., which was done to lighten the men's carrying weight. Vegetables were scarce while in winter quarters and as soon as we were put on march we were watching for a chance to get some. We struck camp before night, and my mess position was on a rocky hill side. I struck out to see what I could find while the balance of the mess attended to other duties. I did not go far before I was at a cabbage bank, bought two nice heads and returned. The boys had a fire burning, but as the decline in the hill was so great it required staking to keep wood from rolling down. We soon had the camp kettle on, with the cabbage in and each one had his piece of bacon. When it was near done and smelled so good we were sitting on the upper side of the fire, talking of the coming feast. Without warning, one of the stakes had burned and gave away, and as the kettle rolled off down the hill some of the boys tried to catch it, but did not until it stopped, some distance below. Seeing the contents pouring out as the kettle was striking the rocks on its downward course looked so ludicrous that I got to laughing, the balance cursing; and the more I laughed the harder the things they would say of their luck. When they asked me why I laughed, my reply was: "Make the best of a bad thing, as a hearty laugh is healthful," and they replied: "So is cabbage."

We stopped near Fredericksburg and camped there for some time. While in camp I had a severe attack of jaundice, and when the command started to move, I was given a permit of sick leave, so I went into Fredericksburg and took a room at a hotel. I had eaten but little while sick in camp; but the first evening at the hotel I felt somewhat hungry and went to a restaurant and ate an oyster stew. It was not long before I was in bed, suffering greatly, as the oysters would not digest. I was deathly sick for a while, without any aid or relief. During the fore part of the night my door was opened and in stepped provost guard to examine my pass. I lay motionless. The officer in charge had a lantern and as soon as he threw the light on my face he said: "Men, we are not hunting a corpse," and turned and went out. After he had gone I thought I must surely look bad, and he honestly thought I was dead or he would have asked some questions.

I later joined my command near Yorktown. We were now under command of General Magruder,* and here began my service on the front. Magruder had fortified part of his front by putting a levy across a piece of woodland, boggy, flat. This was partly filled with water and made quite a stretch of front that was easily guarded. There was part of a battery stationed to protect it. My first sight of the enemy was crossing the levy and deploying some distance to the front with a large detail. Toops and I were the detail of Company "F," and he and I were in position on an outpost, near center of the line, and about one hundred and fifty yards apart. Our line, from the best I could observe, had both right and left resting on swamp, and was formed as part of a circle. The position was

---

* John Bankhead Magruder resigned his commission in the U.S. Army to join the Confederate Army in 1861.

in the woods, with no opening in sight. After remaining in position some time I grew restless and felt that we would not have a chance to see a Yankee and from my early education I was satisfied they could take a challenge and not resent it on fair terms; for there we were in their line and ready to fight and as they were invaders and hunting a scrap, they were cowards or they would not take a dare. All such foolish ideas as stated, had been thought of a number of times, but along well in the turn of the evening, when my patience was near exhausted, I heard a gun shot to my right and it was quickly followed by others and nearing my position. I was all eyes to the front and before I was aware of it the line had given away to both right and left, so the first shot that I fired attracted fire to my point. I soon saw that I was about to be cut off, so I turned and put in my best licks for the levy, slackening speed now and then to reload; but at each time the whizzing of a few near bullets said "Faster." Some of the Yankees were good runners and by my slackening to load, had gained on me. When I got loaded I dropped behind a log and started to shoot—the bullets were whizzing from front and both sides, and I saw my only chance was to run, for if they could not hit me, they would soon catch me; and from that point to the levy I tore through the brush and over logs, making such a noise that I heard but few bullets. When I came near the foot of the levy I saw the most of the men crossing— there seemed to be no one in charge and were all panic-stricken. Under the impulse of the moment I called "Halt and hold the levy." All the men who were near me about faced and commenced firing; and as soon as the men on the levy heard the command to halt and the firing of those who had halted, they returned, I think, without an exception. We were well protected under the hill by good size trees and we fired at least fifteen minutes before the enemy gave way, but some of them had gotten within less than one hundred yards of us. The enemy were shooting what we supposed to be "explosive bullets," from the noise they made when hitting a tree. I got several shots, but I did not think any of them hit the mark and I soon satisfied myself from the way the enemy could get from one tree to another that they were expert woodmen and called Toop's attention to it, and compared them as reminding me of wild turkeys. I don't think we killed or wounded one, and whilst they made a number of close shots, there was not one of our men hurt.

On returning to camp my remarks were contrary to my education. My words were: "Boys, the impression that we have about the Yanks being poor woodsmen and marksmen will not hold good, if our levy experience is a sample; for I think I am fairly competent to judge. I have fished and hunted a great deal, from a small boy up; I have had the association and advice of both the white man and the Indian in Woodcraft, and I think the Yanks that we fought were as expert getting from one tree or log to the other as ever I saw, and they reminded me in cunningness of wild turkeys; so I think now, if we wing one a piece through our service, we have done a good job, and the thing that now interests me most is to find out where those Yanks are from, and if there are many of them; so boys, let me hear from you, if you hear anything about them." I suppose there was some interest taken in the matter, for in a few days I was informed that they were "Western trappers and Hunters." My reply was: "Thank God for that; for the great odds we will be forced to fight, there would be but few of them."

Toops* was an old acquaintance, and possibly a distant relative of Captain O'Brien, and was in the captain's mess. The captain was a noble specimen of humanity; was very brave, just and kind and open to expression, but thought himself a correct judge of men. It was his hobby that if he had a regiment of such men, calling the names of a number that were in the company, he could accomplish anything in the way of battle that could be done by the same number of men. His idea of a soldier was the wild, reckless, camp-fighter, the ones the "slow pokes" would have to guard when in the guard house; so I with quite a number of others was classed as an all around good camp man and would fight in battle line with the others to lead. It was not long after we returned to camp before one of the boys said to me: "Bill, I heard Toops tell the captain that he had thought him a good judge of a soldier, but now he questioned it and he thought before we got through he would be of the same opinion."

As we were camped some distance to the rear, we heard but little from the front, so we passed quite a time in drilling and camp duties, with plenty of rations, but vegetable food was very scarce, less wild onions; and I think they were the most plentiful and the largest I ever saw, but one hearty meal of boiled bacon and wild onions will satisfy one's craving for vegetables for some time.

In the course of time, Magruder's forces commenced to move—of course, we knew nothing of the why and wherefore of such moves; but it was only a short time until we had a

---

* *Hood's Texas Brigade: A Compendium*, compiled by Colonel Harold B. Simpson, lists on page 216, "Demosthenes Toups . . . a native Frenchman: Detailed as a regimental butcher . . . Toups was the French cousin of Captain W. D. Williams, the Co. Cmdr."

brush with the enemy. There was considerable rifle practice by both sides, but little damage was done. The enemy shelled the woods liberally with what the "knowing ones" called "mortar guns" from their boats. I know the shells were large and made a frightful sound as they passed over us and exploded beyond. The 1st Texas Regiment had a company with quite a number of Indians enlisted and from what I learned, they protested against such warfare, as the fellow who shot those big guns was out of reach of their rifles, and they were not having an equal show. I think this ended the Indians' service, as I understand they were sent back home.

I, with a number of others, had quite an amusing experience—with a happy ending—and it was this: We were sufferers from camp diarrhea, as it was called, and up to that time we had found no cure. So, entering the battle, I had quite a great fear that something disgraceful might happen and it was somewhat uppermost in my mind; but to my surprise the excitement, or something else, had effected a cure. I inquired of some of the others and they reported a cure.

From this point we moved slowly towards Richmond, with but little happening worth mention—only the shortage at times of rations, and the pangs of hunger. A little parched corn at times was very acceptable, and I never will forget the issuance of a pint of corn meal each, and my cooking it into mush, without salt to season it. It smelled so good that I was tempted to eat before it was done, and of all the morsels I had eaten before or since, I enjoyed it most. Our marching ended near Richmond, at the Chickahominy Swamp. Here we saw some hard service; but had plenty to eat. Here was where I saw my first balloon ascension. The enemy made a daily practice on some part of their front, taking observations, but they were hauled down in a hurry after a shot or two had been fired at them from our field artillery. The country that we here operated in was rather level and at places swampy, and at times part of it was covered with water. I well remember one experience on our picket line that crossed a railroad that ran into Richmond. The detail that I was in was picketing from the railroad, a short distance to the left, and the position was a disagreeable one; and on account of water we were forced to floor the ground with cord wood to keep out of water, when attempting to sleep. This made rather an uncomfortable pallet, with the spread of a blanket. Through ignorance, or design—I never knew which—we had to be on duty two hours on and two off; so this gave but little time for preparing food or sleeping, and was very wearying. But probably for the best, as stopping longer might have caused sickness as we were, of necessity, partly wet. The enemy at this point had a locomotive on the track with a small cannon mounted on the tender and a few sharp-shooters concealed so they would enliven that part of the picket line by backing in as near us as was safe and giving us a load of grape or shell and a round or two from their concealed sharp-shooters. We were only kept at this point twenty-four hours, but were well worn out when we reached camp. In one of our reconnoitering trips at this place we pressed well to the front and had to wade water at times, with bullets flying. This was the first time that our captain had a fair opportunity to test his "pet soldiers," as we "pokes" called them. The most desperate ones of his "pets" made the worst showing. One of them in particular was so scared and in the way that he should have had our pity; but on the contrary, all who showed the "white feather" heard of it then and there in rough words; so the captain heard for himself. Soon after that, he said to me that he thought he was a good judge of human nature, but now he realized that he knew but little, as our campaigning up to that time had proved too many misjudging.

We remained in and around Seven Pines* for quite a while, with considerable skirmishing at times. At this place, and where a stray bullet might be expected at any time, I got my first sight of President Davis,† accompanied by Judge Reagan‡ and others. Being in the swamp so much, had to some extent water-sobbed our feet, which was felt afterward. While at this place the regiment was one day near the front and held ready for a moment's notice. The picket line was a short distance to the front, and from all appearances the place had been occupied by troops for some time, and by some who were very lousy; for lice could be seen crawling on the grass leaves and body of the trees. Here I learned that in moving and occupying the same grounds occupied by others, that cleanliness was no bar to lice. The color of the Confederate uniform had the advantage over the Federal in not showing them when on the outside of the clothing. One now in civil or military life is apt to think that the men's often lousy condition was due to lack of individual effort. This was the case to some extent; but would not hold good under most conditions, as in hard and long campaigning, often with no change of clothing until worn off the body and probably for weeks without washing and then often with little chance of boiling. I suppose the lice pest is far greater in infantry than in other branches of the service. I guess by this time there would be some method of ridding a lousy pair of pants and

* Seven Pines was south of Richmond on the James River.
† Jefferson Davis was the president of the Confederate States of America.
‡ John H. Reagan was the postmaster general of the Confederacy.

shirt, and not do as we did. Our plan was, when they got so thick that they were hardly bearable, to make a fire of a small amount of straw or leaves and hold the garment over the blaze and from the heat they would drop off, be burned, or be ready for the next fellow. If one was well stocked with big fat fellows, it would remind him of popping corn. The uneducated may think I have said too much for truth of this subject; but if he or she will ask some old "battle-scarred soldier" he will give you a few lines more.

Gen. Jackson's Flanking Gen. McClellan and Seven Days' Battle Before Richmond, Virginia

<hr>

In THE COURSE of time we were ordered to prepare to move, so we were marched to Richmond and boarded a train and ran up to Stanton. There were but two incidents of note. The train that I was on broke from the engine on a long down grade between Richmond and Lynchburg and the experience of my indescribable feeling with the train of flat cars, well packed with men, going at high speed and the engine keeping out of the way, is well imprinted on my memory. We changed to box cars at Lynchburg and passed through a long tunnel, before arriving at Stanton. The tops of the cars were well strewn with men when we entered the tunnel and we had to lie down and flatten out, but the feeling of insecurity was felt in entering, for there appeared but little room between the roof and top of the tunnel. There were reported two men crippled and one of them with a broken leg. We arrived at Stanton and remained a few days. Learned that chestnut rails were the only safe fencing in time of war, as they were a poor thing to make fire with which to cook by.

From Stanton we were carried some distance by rail then

marched across a rough, hard road country—here is where our soft feet suffered. My old friend A. N. Vaughn* of Company "F" suffered tortures on the march, as one of his heels had blistered so badly nearly all the thick skin under the heel had separated from the foot, but with all the persuasion and abuse that I could bring to bear, he would not drop out of rank. He would say: "Bill, I have unfortunately been sick at each fight and the boys will soon take me to be a coward, and I would prefer death than to be looked upon in that light; and there is no use of you saying any more, as I have made up my mind to go into the next fight if I wear off to my knees." So with that set determination he stuck seven days of it that I think were sufficient to dispel all his fear.

On our march we found that we were under Stonewall Jackson, and from that we supposed (from the direction we were moving) we were flanking General McClellan, which proved to be the case. About twelve hours before striking the enemy, I was ordered to select a man and report to General Jackson to the front. I selected a Charles McCauley,† a young man who had only resided in Beaumont a short time before enlisting. "Mc" was of great vital force, ever active and courageous; was educated as a civil engineer and at a glance could take the lay of the surroundings and was a fast runner. When we reported, our orders were to move to the front of the advance guard. This we did, with the general riding close

---

* Archibald Nicholas Vaughan was the owner/editor of Beaumont's first newspaper, the *Beaumont Banner*. A generation later, his daughter Florence married Bill's son Harvey Davis. They were the parents of Bill's namesake and constant companion, William Andrew Fletcher II.

† The Precinct 5 Sabine Pass census of July 10, 1860, lists a civil engineer named C. McCally. This is also the way it is spelled in *Hood's Texas Brigade: A Compendium*.

behind so we were not challenged. Some distance ahead we received our instructions, which were: To proceed cautiously, keeping just out of sight of advance guard and flankers, and to report to him if the enemy were sighted or any sign of them. We proceeded in this way for some time—part of the time the general was with us and other times he was a short distance behind. The country that we were in was timbered, with now and then an opening, and to keep as directed, it was necessary to mend our pace when we saw an opening that we were to pass through, so we would be on the opposite side, or rather out of sight when the advance entered the opening. At a point of this kind, we discovered a burning bridge on the opposite side. A glance was all that it took to satisfy us to make a correct report, so "Mc," as I called him, and I double-quicked back, but did not have to go far before we met the general. We reported and made good time back with the general to the point of observation. He, taking in the situation instantly, ordered us to cross the stream and investigate some distance beyond; and, looking well to both sides of the road, we went forward at fast time and found the stream to be a sluggish, boggy drain, about thirty feet wide, with good high banks. We crossed about two hundred yards above the bridge, nearly dry footed and went forward in the direction to strike the road about four hundred yards from the bridge; were traveling hurriedly, and nearing the road, when we discovered a line of "blue coats," not being over thirty yards of them, near their right flank. We halted instantly and they ordered us to come in, with a few guns pointing our way. I said "run," and we sure did—they never fired a shot. When we struck the creek we did not look for a favorable crossing, but made a leap and landed well in the mud, nearly waist deep. We scrambled across and were on the home side in short order. Just then I saw a straggling Yankee who had been up to a farm house and was making his way back to the bridge to cross, not knowing it had been fired. He was not over fifty yards off and as I saw him first I levelled my gun and ordered him to "trot in." He obeyed promptly. I pointed the direction and told him to trot on ahead. The general was where we left him and it seemed he had anticipated his needs, for there was a battery at the rear, just in sight, with a clear track. I had no more than gotten through reporting, when the battery came forward in quick time and were in line for firing. When the officer in charge of the battery reported, the general called him by name and said: "Fletcher, instruct as to point of enemy's location and return and investigate, and report the effects of firing."

I did as instructed and there was soon a rain of shell pouring in on their position. The battery was well elevated and "Mc" and I were making fast time under their firing. The battery ceased firing as we crossed the stream and went into the woods; found the enemy had gone, and from the looks of the battery work, their position was well shelled. When we returned we reported all clear. There was a force of men putting out the smouldering fire and filling the stream up with logs and other material near at hand. The work was soon completed and the delay in moving was shorter than one would have supposed, as quick time seemed to be the order of the day. I had heard of forced marching and was satisfied that I was in one, for from the time that we left Stanton, men were moved at the full speed of endurance and after "Mc" and I went to the front, the speed we traveled to keep as directed, would give one an idea that the nearer our approach was to the enemy, the faster was our march.

After passing the burned bridge, the country up to the

time we struck the enemy, was the same as that we had passed that day, but with less openings. The woods were well under brushes and we could see but a short distance, only in straight parts of the road. After crossing the stream, the general stayed close up with "Mc" and I the balance of the time we were with him. After we had gone some distance we came to a road that intersected ours on the right. Here we were halted and in less than five minutes the cavalry came up; so as it were, our cavalry and infantry had joined forces. The cavalry halted and the general had a few words with the commanding officer. We moved on, but did not go over one-fourth of a mile when the general halted us and instructed that we travel some little distance to the right of the road, as only a short distance ahead there was an opening and he thought that we would see the enemy's pickets. I asked that, if we did, should we shoot and he replied, "Yes." So as "Mc" and I turned out of the road the general turned back. We made our way quickly to the edge of the opening, about fifty yards from the road, and as expected, there were the cavalry pickets about one hundred and fifty yards out in the opening. Just then there was an officer whom we took to have the rank of "colonel," who seemed to be inspecting the picket line and had, what we supposed to be, two "orderlies" with him. I whispered to "Mc" to fire as I did. In a few moments the opportune time had arrived and there were two reports, near as one. He reeled to one side just as his aides caught him; but by the time we had reloaded, the picket line were all out of shooting distance, and our cavalry was thundering by on a charge. Less than half a mile ahead our cavalry ran into the picketing reserve, and from the appearance, where they were camped, there must have been a regiment. "Mc" and I moved on to where the cavalry were fighting, but before we reached the point, the enemy were falling back—from the firing, our men were in close pursuit. We stopped here to wait for our command as we knew our mission was finished. We waited until nearly dark before our command came up. The cavalry continued skirmishing till dark. We struck camp just before dark, in sight of the skirmishers.

During the night there was what was called a "loose horse." This sometimes happens when a horse is under great excitement, and may be from either side, when the combatants are at close quarters. At the instant the horse is sighted, the words "loose horse" are heard and will be repeated by hundreds of voices along the line, although the animal may pass directly through the camp to the rear, the whole encampment has been notified. In this instance the horse passed quartering through camp and about fifty yards to the rear of where I had been sleeping. I know of no words that will bring the sleeping soldiers to their feet as quickly as "loose horse," for everyone feels the necessity of clearing the track. The word "whoa" is a very popular one as the horse is passing through, but the users know it will have no effect on the distracted animal and would be about as much heeded as if directed at a whizzing cannon ball.

The next morning we were in line by the time one could see, and moving to the front. I soon saw that we were the reserve, which is a dreaded position when kept up for you will hear the roar of the battling front; see the wounded going and being carried to the rear; and if advancing, as we were in this instance, passing the dead and dying, and being exposed to shell, or grape, or cannister shot; moving, standing or lying down, it is all the same—one may be shot down and not so much as raise a hand in self defense; and as one has ample time for reflection, they can well feel the seriousness of the surroundings with all its horrors and to see the little regard for human life and property so victory and the lauding of a few can be attained. As a man becomes more aged and has bettered his reasoning, the clearer insight he has to the great danger of unreasoned public agitation. Along in the turn of the evening the battle was raging and from the roar to our right, it seemed to be a general engagement. The reserve, as far as I could see, was keeping close up to the battle front. As our column was moving to the right there were two men in front of me of Company "F" who had become terror stricken and were retarding the quick time close-up move that we were making. They could not stand erect or move with a courageous bearing, but were dodging and stooping, which often caused an unnecessary gap. This caused me several times to speak harshly to them. I well remember my last words to them, which were: "Boys, straighten up; you are giving them damned Yankees two chances by stooping, as a shell that would pass in front without injury would cut your heads off, bent as you are." The words had not been uttered many seconds when a cannon ball had struck each near the shoulder and tore the bodies badly.

Company "F" near this point was detached from the column and moved to the left as flankers. The reserve was soon thrown into action, relieving those who had been battling for some time at a hard contested point. When Hood's Brigade went into action, they raised the Texas yell, and the "F" boys full well knew its meaning was "charge." Captain O'Brien kept Company "F" to the left a few hundred yards and advanced, as sound indicated, so as to retard or report flank movement if attempted by the enemy. Our progress at times was slow as we were in a piece of woodland that had suffered greatly from cannonading, and there were places we had to surround on account of fallen brush which showed it had been a point of note for field artillery. In this timber I suppose was the enemy's right, as our forces in going in, cut off a regiment. This regiment had a curious position or alignment to me that I did not understand at the time, nor since—why a line of battle should be formed with a detached regiment at right angles and apparently giving no heed to the giving to the rear of their battle line. While Company "F" was moving rapidly in quite a depression, the bullets were coming thick and fast, but no enemy in sight. The company was ordered to lay down and I was ordered to investigate. From the firing where the company was situated, I was satisfied the enemy was firing at right oblique. I went forward so as to flank them, and looking to my right I saw two of our soldiers going quick time to the front of enemy's lines. The idea that flashed through my mind was, that they were poor in woodcraft or they would not have so exposed themselves. My idea of the enemy's position proved correct, for when I reached the top of the elevation, to my right, I saw their line, and as I saw nothing to prevent and the conditions favorable for a close inspection, I cautiously but quickly made the move so I was a little to the rear and about one hundred yards from their right flank. Taking in the situation quickly, I started to raise my gun to shoot the colonel, as he was on the right of the column; but as shooting only in self-defense would have been advised on a reporting mission, I turned, running, and had well struck down grade before I was observed. Being on down grade I felt reasonably safe while I kept up my speed, for I well knew that in favorable conditions a large percentage of the bullets would pass over. I came near falling twice on my plunge downward, as I was nearly tripped up by fallen limbs; and it seemed that the whole line was obliquely firing in my direction. When I reached the point where I had left the company I saw that they were gone, or I had headed wrong; so I jumped behind a tree for protection and scanned the surroundings for the company, and not seeing them, was satisfied that they had moved; so I moved on at quick time in the supposed direction of the company's travel. This I was correct in, for after I had gone some distance double-quicking, I ran onto our orderly sergeant. I asked where the company was and he said they were mostly ahead, but badly scattered. We were then passing near a tented commissary department, which, from appearances, was well stocked with food. Just then to the right and two or three hundred yards ahead, I saw our line forming and directly to my right about seventy-five yards I saw a tall "Yankee" well bent in a long trot, and passing through the tented ground, in an effort, I suppose, to escape. I said, as I raised my gun, "Look, ser-geant," and the words were not more than said when I fired—the man dropped his gun, staggered to the right and fell. The sergeant said, "You got him," and I remarked that he had quit his gun, at least. At this time firing had about ceased on the extreme left of Lee and right of McClellan. The density of the smoke a few feet above the earth was so great that it obscured the sun. When I reached the forming line I saw what the Texas Brigade had done, for only a short dis-tance to the front was what was once one of the enemy's batteries, and if memory serves me right, there were six pieces. Just as I reached my forming company, the regiment that I have mentioned came running in without order and shooting some; and a man by the name of "Wood" of "F," fell mor-tally wounded, being shot in the back. The boys about faced and some of them fired. This caused the enemy to well un-derstand their condition and they surrendered. The colonel of the enemy's regiment and the 5th Regiment's Lieutenant Colonel Upton,* I learned, were schoolmates. The Yankee colonel felt abused for the rude and unmilitary way he had to surrender, as a private soldier disarmed him, and he felt humiliated. I was told that when he and Upton met he complained of his abuses of not being allowed to turn his arms over to an officer. Upton replied: "You did the right thing," for his men understood war to be kill or capture, and understood capture was not complete until the enemy was disarmed; and they recognized no difference between private or officer.

As soon as our lines were formed, we were ordered to lay down, as the picket lines were posting and there was some firing and a passing bullet now and then made the position a disagreeable one. Soon after dark there was a detail made of three from a company to go to the rear and get rations for the company. I was one of "F" detail, but the detail received no orders to report to officer, or where to go; only to go to the rear and get rations, so we made our way to a point not far to the rear, where we had seen the commissary. When we arrived at the place there were a number of details with orders similar to ours and no effort being made to load up. I inquired what the trouble was and was told that we could get rations only with a written order, as there was a guard over them. "F" detail went to where one guard was stationed and I asked him why we could not get rations and he explained, as stated. I tried to reason with him, telling him the men

---

* William Felton Upton was born in 1832 in Franklin County, Tennessee. He moved to Fayette County, Texas, in 1859, where he farmed until war broke out. He served in Hood's Texas Brigade during the entire Civil War.

were very hungry, and if they did not let us have the supplies, there might be trouble. I saw from his dress that he was no regular and asked him where he was from. He said his company that were there guarding were the Richmond Home Guards, and were there to protect captured goods. I saw from the tone of expression of the details, that all that was needed was a leader, so I backed off a short distance, (it being dark), so the source would not be known and spoke in a loud tone of voice commanding: "Fix bayonets and be ready to defend yourselves; take all the rations you want and leave the rest with guard." This command was instantly obeyed, less fixing bayonets, as there were but few in the detail; but the guard was not so well posted and raised no further objections. From what I could hear, each man was loading up and calling out his find, so by that means we were soon posted and got a good assorted supply, with what bottled whiskey we wanted as extra. When we returned to the company we found the men still lying down, but when we reported full handed they all sat up and ate, and from the way the bottles were passed back and forth, one now would think they had never heard of "prohibition." So, with a full stomach, we passed the balance of the night in battle line, or what is termed sleeping on your arms, which means not undressing; not so much as to even remove knapsack or haversack.

The next morning we were up and ready for duty, the firing in our immediate front having ceased, so we were not held strictly under a moment's notice order, therefore, it was nearly impossible under such conditions to keep a volunteer body under strict discipline, and there was a percentage that would be to the rear; some through curiosity, others looking for some dead, wounded or missing friend or relative through this channel. It was reported that the officer in charge of the

Richmond Guards had reported to General Jackson about the taking of the supplies without written orders, by men who claimed to be detailed and the reply of Jackson was, that all they needed belonged to them, as they had taken it; so that settled any fear of the detail being punished.

Now, I will retrace my steps of the following evening and will make what would have been my report to Captain O'Brien had he not moved Company "F," and I will give further the impression formed. As I have before stated, I reached my company while forming, and all minds were absorbed, especially the officers' in getting the men back to their places from their scattered position through a closely contested fight, and that on a charge is one of the officer's most important duties; so seeing this condition, I waited until matters were somewhat quiet before I approached the captain. When I did, my words were: "Captain, I suppose a report now is useless." His reply was: "Yes, but little did I expect to see you again. I was forced to move the company, as the position was too hazardous." My reply was: "I guess they were shooting at me." His words were: "I thought so, and they would aim lower as you descended." My report would have been: I gained a position a little to enemy's rear and about one hundred yards to the right there was a regiment on the brow of a ridge, facing and firing. They were formed nearly parallel to the hollow we passed in and I saw, near their center, a barrel on end and men passing to and from. I supposed it was whiskey, and from the battle line our forces now occupied they were cut off and I was fearful through a drunken condition they would try to force an escape and cause uncalled for killing. Commenting, I will state, that when I saw the enemy's position on the hill, I could not understand it; and up to this date have not figured it out, as they were near at right angles to their battle line, facing out and only a few hundred yards to the right. If they had been facing the opposite direction and went into battle, as our relief charged, they would have struck them directly on the left and rear flank and, with a well directed enfilading fire,* done great damage and brought about such confusion as would have made our charge unsuccessful; and as Company "F" passed about two hundred yards to their front, I would not have been sent forward to investigate if they had not been firing in that direction; and further, if our left had extended a regiment or two further, they would have been at the same disadvantage that they could have placed us in.

I will now proceed where I left off at detail punishment. We were soon formed and commenced moving off of what I afterwards learned was "Gaines Farm." We spent the next few days tramping after a defeated foe, but not brought into action. We were in the rear and yet, I supposed, as reserve. I only saw two points of mention—one where reports said we had a division posted to cut off McClellan's retreat, that the men were held in position and let his army pass without firing a gun. This, of course, brought forth a universal expression of condemnation of the officer in charge.

The next was pleasing to the sight and pleasant for reflection. In passing near the end of a narrow but good length opening, there lay evidence of a masterly piece of marksmanship—blue coats with bodies enclosed, lay in line for some distance, and so close that it put one in mind of a railroad grade with ties laid for ironing. The sight may have been awful to behold to some, but the fellows in this case who did

---

* "Enfilading fire" pertains to being in a position to rake enemy lines with gunfire in a lengthwise direction.

the viewing wanted to see others, and if there was a proportionate number wounded there were but few sound ones left of the battle line. From the position of the dead, it looked to be the work of one volley, and they lay as if falling with but few struggles. It was reported to be night work with our men, but a short distance to the front.

The next point of interest reached was Malvern Hill. Here we formed in line and I with two others of Company "F" were sent to the front with a large detail. We were posted under the brow of a hill, near the enemy's picket line. While going in we passed a dead "Reb" behind a large tree who had been killed by a cannon ball passing through the tree, although from the size of the tree it looked impossible for a ball to have passed through unless the tree was hollow, and if such was the case, none of us could discover it. Our position was a good one and the enemy's was the reverse, as they were in an open field, with wheat not over two feet high, and thin. Their distance was about three hundred yards less at a point in a narrow hollow. The enemy's battle line was under the brow of a hill in a piece of woods and was nearly at right angles from us; and to their front was a long open field of good width. To our left front in an opening was a battery, about a quarter of a mile off—it was behind their battle line and firing liberally at our troops. About half a mile back, as I have stated, our position was a good one, and I have often thought that the scout who found and reported it would do to tie to, and I suppose it was investigated at night.

The detail was deployed so that they covered about three hundred yards of front and were driven from their position five or six times during the day, and at each time we were driven back and re-took our position, our ranks thinned until we were not more than a dozen strong at night. When we had taken our position we were ordered to silence battery, and we surely did, and it was great fun for the "Rebs" to see the battery boys getting off under the sound of the rebel yell. When the battery was silenced, we would turn our attention to their picket line and what fine shooting it was, for we had a safe position, while they had as exposed a one as I ever saw men in—it looked like replacing the dead and wounded with live men to be slaughtered, with little hope of retaliation. When the battery was silenced, the enemy's right regiment would come from their hiding and fire volley after volley into the woods and the "Rebs" would run for dear life a few hundred yards back and take shelter behind trees and stay hid out, as it were, until the Yankees had gotten their satisfaction of shooting and retired. At each time the regiment advanced, they would remove their wounded, repost pickets and leave one or two sharpshooters at the brow of the hill, and the battery would take position and wake the "Rebs" to rear up. They would some times try to dislodge us by a few rounds of grape shot but were unsuccessful, for they were soon put to flight. Field artillerymen are somewhat like cavalrymen about a horse, and that is, they have formed an attachment as part of their equipment; and to move battery a few wounded horses would have the desired effect. When the Yankees had time to get their horses to protection before we regained our position, the boys had to be well pelted before they would cease firing. I could not tell from the distance the battery was from us, the amount of damage inflicted, but we could soon create quite a commotion and a run to the rear and the changing of or dropping out of horses which we supposed were wounded. I don't think we shot down one of the battery boys, although we may have wounded some. I guess we about accomplished the desired aim without inflicting much damage and our boys in battle line had a much needed rest and nap. As I have stated, our number gradually grew less and after our second advance we were, so far as I knew, without an officer. The remaining men continued doing as first directed and would advance and maintain position at front, at will, and as we could walk well protected a short distance behind our firing line, I would change positions now and then to points that I could best shoot. I don't think there were many of the detail killed or wounded, and the gradual lessening of number was caused by those who did not enjoy the sport, and needed official control.

When I enlisted in the service, my brother* was very anxious to enlist in the same company. I objected and gave him my reasons for objecting, which were: In the first place, I wished to be as far from home and relatives as possible, with but little advantages of hearing from them, for they were poor and could not render me any aid; and as I cast my lot so as to be dependent upon the government, I thought it best to feel at home and be satisfied among strangers, and the greater the distance and the poorer the chance to return I thought would, to a great extent, make me feel as though I were at home in the army; and further, would we not, as brothers, have an attachment, as such, that would often cause worry where there was no chance of aid; and, further, there would be times when one or the other might neglect duty in some vain effort to satisfy some supposed mishap and pass many restless nights when rest was needed, and out of the other's power to render aid. So I asked him to enlist when his services would be needed west of the Mississippi River, which he did. I mention this to show what one is liable to be drawn into

---

* Stephen Benton Fletcher was three years younger than Bill.

through a brotherly feeling. In this detail there were two brothers, both nice, genteel, courageous boys. Along in the turn of the day, when our squad was small and on the advance after having been driven back, and about one hundred yards from the position we had been occupying, to my right about fifty feet was one of these brothers, and to his right about the same distance was the other. The brother near me fell wounded and called to his brother for help, who responded promptly, without apparent thought of what chances he was taking under the worst conditions, for it was evident that he was shot down by a sharpshooter who had been posted to shoot through that opening in the woods. I still advanced, but would cast a glance at the wounded man. The brother was quickly at his side and was bending as though he was going to put his hands on him—he staggered and fell, I think, before his hands touched his brother. The sharpshooter had gotten two from the same position, which would not likely have happened under other conditions. If this had occurred in battle line, the helping one would have weakened the battling force two; but happening as it did, the loss was less felt. The brother did not consider the near position of a good marksman with an opening through brush that he could have held only a few minutes longer, as he would have made a target for both right and left of our line, and being of that class that always figures well on self protection, and his whereabouts then was located, he was only holding his ground for a minute, expecting what happened.

We soon evened up in numbers, however under nearly the same conditions, for just to the left of the position which we had been occupying was a narrow hollow pointing to our left front, and just before we were driven back, I noticed from the report of a gun that there was some one in it, so in going forward I made for the mouth of the hollow which extended out left a short distance. The left post man and I were understood so when I crawled to the desired point and raised up, I saw, somewhat to my surprise, a Yankee on his knees facing me, with his gun leaning on a low worm-rail fence, with his arms on the fence and his head bowed down as though he was napping. He was not more than seventy-five yards distant. I fired quickly. He called piteously, "Oh, Pat! Oh, Pat! I am shot, come here!" Pat reached him while he was moaning. Pat looked to be a spare built boy, about of age. I had beckoned the man near and he was at my side, and just as Pat had reached his friend, he fell by a bullet at the hands of the man I had beckoned; so, in the space of thirty minutes there were two Yankees shot similar to the two brothers.

The closing scene of the day on that part of McClellan's line was the grandest sight, to me, of the war. Just as it was darkening, the "Rebs" emerged in an open field, in line of battle, about four hundred yards to the right and front of our position, and as they were at right angles from us and when the enemy's position was observed, we found them in the same alignment and were just at the edge of the opening under the brow of the hill, in the piece of timber that I have mentioned where the enemy hid from view that had driven our outpost in several times during the day. Just as our men had gotten near the middle of the opening, the enemy 'rose up and turned loose a volley. Instantly our troops replied, and the two streams that went forth were grand to behold. Our men then charged, and a stream of fire far down the line poured forth from both sides. This sight was awe-inspiring and a happy ending, as the enemy soon gave way, so we then headed for camp, with my part played in the great drama of the seven days' fight before Richmond. My cartridge box, however, was empty and I was well satisfied with the days' rifle practice. I suppose the enemy had removed at each time they passed over their picket line dislodging us, their wounded, as we never shot a helpless wounded. At each time we re-posted there was none in sight, but some of the boys the next morning claimed that they counted sixty odd dead, being the work of the detail.

Leaving this place, we were marched back to Richmond, with only two incidents. I will mention the first which was with a tobacco peddler. This character of people are generally on to their job. They expect, from the way the most of them act, that all goes and is permissible in war, as some of them are as well versed in sharp practices as some soldiers are. At this time we were out of chewing tobacco and the peddler was near the road, and from appearances, had a rush of customers; and it was permissible in such cases for a few to drop out of line of each company as they were passing to supply their wants. I had dropped out and was crowding in when I observed one of Company "F" boys to my front. I pushed a five dollar Confederate bill to his front and requested that he get me some. He turned his head and seeing who it was, said: "Keep your money." He soon got in place and stood there, what I thought was an unnecessary length of time, while the others were getting their orders filled, and change, if any was coming. I finally heard him give his order as though he had made it before and it had not been heeded and as the peddler always exacted cash in advance and handed out change, if any was coming, as he delivered the goods, so he immediately filled the order for five plugs, thinking as I suppose, he had taken the pay. So after filling the order, he went to filling others and my man asked with an oath whether he was to get his change or not. The peddler gave him immediate attention and asked what it was. The reply was: "I handed you ten dollars," and the peddler immediately handed over five dollars. We pushed out and started on—he handed me one plug and remarked, "Bill, here's four more, and five dollars I have left." I asked him why he stood so long before making order. He said: "I wanted to see if he was well supplied with ten dollar bills, so he would not catch up with me." I asked what that had to do with the matter, and he said: "Lots, for I did not have any money."

The next is the sight of passing over and near the battlefield, seeing the destruction that it brought to man, beast and property—here a few graves, there a long line of new earth, the dead thrown in masses, somewhat denoting number—here destruction of commissary's dead animals, vehicles, in fact a part of all that is necessary to equip and give comfort to a large body of men, and the awful stench that at times would greet one's nostrils, and in this instance myriads of flies.

We were placed in camp a few miles from Richmond, and a considerable distance from the battlefield so as not to be affected with the odor but the distance was not so great that it prevented great numbers of flies coming our way that were supposed to have originated on the battlefield. They were something less than the common house-fly, and when they bit or sucked it left a stinging sensation, and when one lay down for a nap in daytime he was forced to cover up, as it were, head and ears. We stayed in this camp quite a while, resting, and our ranks were strengthened by a number of recruits from Liberty and Jefferson County, Texas. We passed off the time very well and roamed the country near by, at will, when not on duty; but were prohibited from going into

Richmond without a pass, and from disobedience of this order I served my first and last sentence in the guard house, or any other character of punishment for disobedience of orders. Company "F" at this time was in charge of the first lieutenant, and he was at this camp rather exacting of some; and I suppose it was caused by their disrespect and probable remarks, although I had made none; but he was satisfied that I had often been in position to see his weakness. I applied to him twice for a pass to go to Richmond after well explaining my mission, but was denied. One of my near neighbor boys and schoolmate, and the brother of my sister's husband,* lay seriously wounded in the hospital—he belonged to a Louisiana regiment. He sent me word that as soon as he was able he would get a furlough, and as his wound was through his breast and lung, he guessed he would not be able to do any more fighting; and he would like to see me once more, as we had not met for years; and my anxiety was great to send my sister some word. I determined to disobey orders, so the next morning I went to one of the boys who had a pass for the day and explained conditions and asked his assistance in passing the picket guard line and that I would risk the city patrol. So we went to near picket guard and selected a favorable place. He passed on through and I went down to a point selected in front of the guard and he in the rear. His pass landed, tied to a rock, at the proper place in front of the picket line. I picked it up and he and I continued on our course, passing a few guards. I entered and returned the pass and we went on to Richmond, parting as we entered the suburbs. As I was fairly well posted on the lay of the city and

---

* Mary Elizabeth Fletcher married Austin Allen of Opelousas, Louisiana, on May 18, 1854.

position of the hospital, I passed through the suburbs to avoid patrol which was mostly in density of the city. Knowing the hospital was well out on the opposite side of the city, I feared no interference. Reached the hospital O.K., stayed till nearly dark and returned to camp, for there was no challenge made by picket guard, going in. The next morning I was put in the guard house and served sentence for not being at evening roll call. In a few days, Captain O'Brien returned and was, through some channel or other, informed; and from what I was told, he expressed his feelings to the lieutenant in very forcible words, disapproving his sentence. The captain said that when men had earned consideration as I had, it was brutal to deny, for they never asked when services were needed.

Our nearness to the city gave us a good number of peddlers daily, both from country and city, and as there was no "pure food" law in force we bought about everything that was offered, without question, if it suited our taste or fancy. Sausage was one of our favorite dishes, and as the vendors were on hand in considerable numbers early in the morning, we had sausage on the bill of fare when desired. So one morning, while our mess was eating, I found what I supposed was a cat's claw and all stopped eating at once and an examination was hurriedly made of the uneaten portion, and a cat's tooth was discovered. A report of the find was soon circulated and it was said that there were other finds of a similar character. Sausage was sold by weight and the more bone, the heavier. This was practicing "all things are fair in war." Some of the boys tried to vomit, but the cat kept on its downward course, so there was a slump in the sausage market; and as far as that camp was concerned, no argument could reinstate sausage and it soon was not wanted, therefore, was not an article offered.

As one was at liberty to roam the near country when not on duty, but answering at morning and evening roll call, it gave good opportunity for near foraging, as it was called, and as a few miles out was well stocked with ripe wild huckleberries and as I was very fond of them, I made several trips. I would start out in company with one of the boys, each being equipped with a canteen, a pint cup and small amount of sugar, so we would stroll around until we saw a milch cow or cows grazing that were out of sight of house, and if not, we sometimes, in passing, could "shoo" them and they soon were, so when the opportune moment came, one of us would grab the cow by the horns and the other would fill the canteens with milk, then off to the nearest berry patch we would go and partly fill our cup with berries, then sugar and cream same. We would continue this process as often as necessary to fill our stomachs, then return to camp, feeling that we, at least, had eaten unadulterated berries and milk. The cattle were generally good milkers and the most of them very gentle, and I guess, from the number of boys who finally caught on, the milk maids at least thought some of their cows were drying up. This good thing did not last a great while, however, for the owners took to keeping the cattle in sight or under herder, and when milk was not at hand, we did very well on berries and sugar. A short distance out of camp there was a macadamized pike* with toll gate just before entering the city limits, and late in the evening there were a great number of huckster cars or wagons passing into the city. I heard that it was amusing to watch the boys and the hucksters, so I took a good position near the pike for observation. At different

* A "macadamized pike" is a road made by compacting layers of small broken stones into a convex, well-drained roadbed.

places on the roadside the soldiers could be seen—lying down, walking, or playing—all seemed to be out for an airing. When the vehicles would pass going in slow trot, often in numbers, one or two of the soldiers would drop in behind the vehicle and take such market products as could be reached, the driver, of course, looking ahead, while the driver in the rig behind would laugh and enjoy the sport of seeing his neighbor robbed—when the same thing was happening at the rear of his cart. It was surprising to see the amount of truck taken in this way, and it seemed to be so amusing to the driver behind that he lost all thought of his load and was all eyes to the front; and from the great number of vehicles passing, there was quite a lot of foraging done in this way. It was several evenings before the hucksters caught on, after which they were watchful and this broke up the soldiers' profit and sport. I remember hearing some of the boys say that some of those old fellows put them in mind of an owl turning its head without moving its body.

In this camp we had plenty to eat and were soon rested up and fattened so we could stand a long hard drive to the next slaughter pen. Leaving this camp, we were marched over the country, and from the privates' point of view, we were hunting a fight. We did fairly well for food and when the commissary department was short we would add roasting-ears and green apples to the bill of fare; although the latter were green, but were considered eatable by us, as the bloom was off. It sure was a blessing that our stomachs had gotten near, as is said of the ostrich. I well remember at one time on this tramp, Company "F" was detached from the regiment and stationed in a cornfield, near a stream. There could, at times, be seen some "Yanks" on the opposite side of the stream, but there was no shooting heard and the company seemed to be held there for an emergency and was kept hid in tall corn which was in roasting-ears. We were all very hungry, but as yet had never made a meal of raw corn. As there was no chance of cooking any, some of the boys started eating and we soon were all feasting, less Captain O'Brien—he would peel the stalks and chew them as one does sugar cane. Some of the boys would joke the good natured old captain and finally got him to partake of the same food as they said he was furnishing them, as they saw no other purpose of our being herded in field but to graze. The corn was of fine large ears and in the right stage of maturity for good eating. We were held at this point for several hours and while there I consumed four ears, and some of the boys did better. There was a large man by the name of Benjamin who ate at least eight or ten ears and the boys would tell it on him and add a bundle of fodder. We were ordered to return to our command just before night and found it a short distance to the rear. When leaving the field, the captain told us to gather what corn we wanted, so I took to camp six ears. When we reached camp we soon had fires burning and the corn in shucks on them cooking, and we found this a quick and excellent way to cook corn as the shucks retain the flavor. We also drew liberally of fine fresh beef and this we also soon had on the fire broiling in good size pieces. All was hurriedly done as we were told that we would take up the line of march soon. When the corn was about cooked and the meat good and hot, but very rare, we were ordered to fall in line. We did so, and the different methods of carrying hot food could not well be described. I partly shucked my ears of corn and carried by the shucks, and the beef on a short stick. It was near dark and we were marching slowly, and as soon as the food was cool enough I commenced lightening my load to the extent of cob and shuck. From the size of my piece of meat and six large ears of corn I supposed I could have supper and breakfast, but such was not the case; for I could not resist eating the whole of it. When I was through I figured the contents of stomach: four green and six cooked roasting ears and raw beef in proportion. I rather expected some ill effects from gormandizing, but such was not the case, and I guess the preventative was the night's marching. We were generally well supplied with tobacco—if the plug man was not handy we could raid the drying shed and be contented with the pure and unadulterated leaf.

BATTLE OF
SECOND MANASSAS

⊹⟩══⟨⊹

WE FINALLY REACHED a point near and fronting where we entered the battle of Second Manassas, and on the eve of the same day were thrown a considerable distance to the front, or rather making a night attack. I suppose this was done to keep the enemy from fortifying their front, which it did, for we fought over the same ground next day in open field. This was the first and last of my experience attacking the enemy in force at night. There was but little damage done on either side, so far as I knew, for the amount of shooting and mixing. When we went in, we soon ran over their first battle line, and from the number of the enemy that passed to our rear, one would suppose that the capture was large; but from what I learned it was not, as most of them went out on flank or hid and were passed as we went back in the dark. The first line we encountered was on our side of a small stream that I understood was "Bull Run." We crossed the stream and were mixed up with the enemy considerably while they were making their way to the rear. There was but little, if any, shooting after we crossed the stream, for we were so scattered and it was so dark that it was impossible to distinguish friend or foe, unless you were near arm's length of each other. When we reached the top of the hill, the officer attempted to form line, but not with any view of company or regiment—the command was "Halt, and get in line, men." I suppose some of our officers at least saw what a predicament we were in, and the order to halt and fall in line might have originated from an under officer or private. All was confusion and could not have been otherwise unless we had formed near the bank of the stream after crossing. When we were halted, near to our front could be seen a dark line of something and in forming. The left of our line or part of the front that I was in, commenced forming on this dark object and those near had seen that it was men, and some "Reb" asked what command it was, and the reply giving the regiment, number and state, was enough to give one the creeps or cold chills. I was only a short distance from the head of the line, and our column was forming at an angle of not over twenty degrees in front of the enemy. The order "about face, march" was instantly given and promptly obeyed, and as far as I was concerned, and I suppose others who heard the name of the regiment felt somewhat as I did and that was walk off quickly but lightly, and keep heart from thumping loud for fear of detection. It sure was fortunate for us that the enemy did not ask first what command we were, for one well directed volley would have gotten scores of "Rebs" and a few "Yanks," and it was supposed that the enemy had taken us for their reforming front, not knowing that a large percentage of them had laid down and skulked to the rear after being passed over. There was a sigh of relief when we were well down the hill and out of danger of the enemy.

We returned to the point from where we started during

the night and stayed in line of battle the better part of the next day. When I had slept and rested I got a permit to go to the front, but with no special mission to fill; it was purely to satisfy individual curiosity, and as I could under certain conditions get a front leave by asking, I made use of it when the spirit moved. While to the front I was at or near our picket right and went some distance to the right front. While on my rambles I went into one of the enemy's infirmaries near our picket front and flank. I found quite a lot of wounded which was the work of our night raid. They seemed to be well cared for, under the conditions, by their army medical corps and one could tell at a glance that the facilities for such work were superior to ours, but one's thought when seeing the enemy's helpless wounded are far different than when seeing the dead. My thoughts on seeing the dead were without one pang of regret or sorrow; but it was the reverse to see the living suffering. I talked with several of the wounded and they seemed to carry no malice, as some of them remarked: "The Johnnies were doing the same as they had been trying to do." I was somewhat amused, however, with one fine looking, intelligent young fellow, who, from appearances and conversation had lived on the bright side of life; he was on his feet and slowly moving about; he said, "Reb, look what you fellows have done for me. I would rather that bullet had gone through my head, and I guess my girl will hunt another fellow when she hears of it." He seemed to be taking his condition greatly to heart and I thought he had just grounds, therefore, could only sympathize; but there could be no relief in that. While at the front, sitting on top of a worm rail fence, I whittled out what was called a "Kentucky button" for my drawers; the wood was of dried oak, and the button or peg about three-fourths of an inch long and over one-eighth of an inch in diameter; the wood was very hard and firm and the peg had no porous streaks in it. I have minutely described the wood, for in a few hours there was at least half of it driven into me, and I have had the idea ever since that there is a part or the other half still in, as only one-half came out, and the doctors at the time and since whom I have asked in regard to it disagree about flesh healing and closing over a woody substance. I was not out long before I returned to the command. From the noise to the left one would know that there was considerable fighting and that there was apt to be something doing soon and a general attack made by our forces, as I have before stated that in our rambles it looked as though we were hunting a scrap and from what I had seen and heard I supposed we had found sufficient Yanks to give battle. I was not long in line before Jeff Chaison, Benjamin and I were sent to the rear to draw Company "F" rations of bacon that was being issued, and the detail surely appreciated it, as we were very hungry, and it somewhat rested with the detail how they drew in the deal. The quartermaster had a list of numbers of companies, but in such cases there was but little roll call and his reports were not always up to date and sometimes the detail could ring in a few new arrivals or steal something, which was legitimate if not caught in the act; and if one was, near time of battle, he would expect no punishment as there is nothing that will settle up all differences more quickly than one's duty well performed in battle line. The meat was large, fat middlings and "F" detail had been liberally treated, so that when we reported to the sergeant at the company and delivered our bacon, he was told not to consider detail in issuing. He asked no questions, but commenced at once to issue. Jeff, Benjamin and I stepped a short distance off and cut in three parts what we had gotten without price or begging. We had no more than got our meat stowed in our haversacks before we were ordered to fall in line. The company's bacon had not been fully issued, but the boys grabbed it up and divided it the best they could, as we marched to the front. The movement to the front was fast walking, and as we all knew well what was coming from the roar to our left, there could be no mistake, so we were soon near enough in for the shells that were being thrown by the enemy's guns to make us forget bacon and hunger. I merely mention this bacon incident to show how our ill-gotten part of it went. I was soon shot down, Benjamin shortly afterwards was killed, Jeff in his scrambles in crossing Bull Run got his haversack full of water and cut it off. We went in, nearly over the same ground that we passed the previous night. We were just emerging from a piece of woods that had but little underbrush and were well closed up and alignment good; we were closing to left and were obliquing. I was not aware of the enemy's nearness and I don't suppose the officers were; I thought they came from Creek Valley to near the brow of the hill when we were sighted coming in, for the country was open and we could well be seen from the opposite side of the creek where their reserve was stationed, so at a distance of about one hundred and fifty yards the enemy was lying down, and rose up in masses and fired one volley. I and one other member of Hood's Brigade fell wounded. As I was obliquing to the left the bullet rather cut across my bowels and made a long and ugly wound. One of the boys told me that I fell face upward and was laughing. I had always some fear of receiving a wound in the stomach, if ever I was so unfortunate as to get one, and had made a practice of wearing my cartridge box to the front when battling, and in this instance it would have protected me if I had not been obliquing. I suppose when I was struck I fainted, for the first I knew was when I raised to a sitting position and the boys were some distance to the front, shooting and yelling at the fleeing enemy. I could see the dead Yanks, as I supposed them to be, lying thick in the battle line—they were a finely dressed set and made a gaudy-looking corpse. I did not see the enemy when they arose and fired as I guess at the instant I was looking to the left, as we were closing in that direction. I was feeling no pain, but felt somewhat dazed and on looking down I saw a rent in the front of my pants. I soon had cartridge box off and pants unbuttoned and as I saw the wound I lay on my back with the idea that I was shot in the bowels. The grape shot and shell were pouring in thick and fast in our rear, a great number falling short of the intended mark, and it made me hopeful that it would soon put an end to my existence. I turned my head to the enemy, thinking I might be so fortunate as to get a dead shot—they poured around, but none hit. I would raise my head often and see if I could discover any signs of discharge from torn intestines, but could discover none. I had also a horror of famishing, as I had heard that one often died for want of water when bleeding badly. I was trying to locate some water in the rear. The wound at the mouth was not bleeding and never did, more than enough to stain my clothes; but, internally, I supposed it was. I thought possibly that it was for want of food that there was no sign of discharge and it did not take long for all these ideas to flash through my mind, so in a short space of time hope returned and I thought that possibly I was not mortally wounded; then fear was uppermost and I crawled about fifty feet to a well rotted stump, thinking it would protect me from shot. I was not much more than settled behind it when the idea struck me that a grape could go through, so I dragged myself to a good sized tree about one hundred feet off and stayed there some time in a reclining position, with head and shoulders resting against the tree. My pants and drawers were open and well off the wound. I saw quite a number of the finely uniformed Yanks running to the rear, and was satisfied their line of dead was lessening by quite a number. As I lay in this position, looking over my right shoulder and to the rear as far as I could see around the tree, I saw one of the "play dead Yanks" getting to the rear with a revolver in his hand. He would have passed about one hundred feet to my right, if he had kept straight forward. I could see he was a private and I concluded the pistol was taken from some dead or badly wounded officer and that he had it for no good purpose. Oh how I wished for my gun so I could disarm him! The thought had no more than struck me when he caught sight of me and turned from his course and made straight for me in a trot. My wish for my gun was multiplied instantly; I felt sure he was going to end my existence. He trotted up to within a few feet of me and raised the pistol pointing toward my head, but instantly lowered it and gave a low grunting sneer and trotted on—there was not a word spoken. I suppose he glanced at my wound, and either weakened from the sight, or thought he would be doing a humane act if he put me out of mysery. I judged him to be a foreigner of low caste and not long from his native soil. About this time our front was crossing Bull Run and struck the "blue coats," as they called them, and they thought it was the same line that we had attempted to form on when we made the night raid, and from what they saw and heard, the front line was composed of New York Zouaves* and such like; that a fine, showy uniform was at the bottom of their patriotism, as they would not retreat and fight and at the first volley they were either dead, wounded or playing dead, or running like hell; but the "blue coats" on the ridge were a tough set to move, and there was no one that I ever heard speak of it but said that if the Zouaves had stood like men, we would have had a very tough job; and the result might have been different.

In our immediate front, while the battle was roaring across the creek, the litter bearers came in sight across an opening. A pair of them with litter had ventured as far as I was, and I being the first man, was hopeful that I would soon be cared for. They came up and had their litter stretched and lying by my side, and were in the act of helping me on—from the roar and amount of flying grape and shell there must have been a new battery coming into action, and I guess I was in luck that I was not on stretcher, and on their shoulders, for I think they would have dropped me. The first round the battery fired seared them and they did not take time to fold litter, but grabbed it by the same end and were off at speed; and me cursing and calling them all manner of hard names, but did not stop them. The sight was so ridiculous that I could not help laughing. My wound was not hurting a particle, but left hip and leg were paralyzed or deadened. I waited

* The original Zouave group was a tribe of Berbers who lived in the mountains of Algeria. They were recruited into the French army in 1831. They became known for their strict discipline, fighting ability, and exotic uniforms. Elmer E. Ellsworth organized and trained a volunteer militia company patterned after the Zouaves in 1859. He later recruited a regiment of New York firemen who were mustered into the Union service in May, 1861. They were known as the First New York Fire Zouaves. Their colorful uniforms were not suited for field service and were eventually abandoned.

a short time, thinking the litter bearers would return, but as they did not, I concluded to make an effort to get to the rear as the tide of battle might change and I might be a wounded captive; so I pulled myself up, found that I could stand on the wounded side without pain and by taking hold of my pants leg with my hand I found I could slowly move to the rear. I did not go far before a straggler offered help and I accepted. I rested my left arm on his right shoulder and made fair time by hopping with my right foot and dragging the left. In something less than a half mile to the rear I crawled in an ambulance and was carted to the field infirmary. Before reaching the ambulance, however, leaning on my helper, there was a courier passing under apparent horse speed. He was about two hundred feet away and to the right front—a shell struck them and exploded, and there was a scattering of parts of both man and horse, and I took it to be a percussion shot that exploded when hitting. My man gave me a hard wrench and received a cursing for the same. A short distance further on I was somewhat amused but cursing mad. Near in front there was a wash, or gully, in the field and there started a rain of unexploded shell. They were skipping, bouncing and rolling at a lively rate, passing near and on each side of us. My man turned me loose and hid out in the gully and no words that I had at command could move him until the battery ceased shelling in our direction.

Arriving at the infirmary, I was soon stretched on my pallet, and from appearances, I was not first by quite a number. I lay there until the time, I suppose, was well in the after part of the night, with now and then a man passing looking after our wants. There struck me at a point in my hip a sensitive feeling which I was satisfied was the dead coming to life, and it was but a short space of time before I was suffering greatly.

I felt the place and by pressing hard I was satisfied I had located the bullet; and I asked one of the boys to hunt a doctor, as I was suffering greatly. He did so, and said he would come soon. This did not satisfy me, and I asked him to return and insist that I get immediate relief. Three of them reported promptly. They found me laying on my right side. I put my finger to the point and asked them to cut in and get the bullet out. They gave the wound a hurried inspection and felt at point for the bullet, but said they could find none. I stated the dead condition of the hip and when reaction set in, the point I had indicated was the first to be sensitive, and I had pressed hard and had well located the bullet; and I wanted them to cut in and get it out as it was lodged on the hip bone. They hesitated a few seconds and had some words, which I heard; and they were debating the advisability. I broke in by saying: "By doing what I say you will save my life; without it I will die." Without further question they commenced to cut and from the way the knife pulled the muscle, I took it to be very dull, and was expressing my views in very forcible terms when one of them remarked: "If you don't hush up we will leave you." My reply was, "It don't hurt as badly when I am cursing." They were not long in extracting the bullet and our division surgeon remarked: "Your chances are good, with proper care; but at first I thought different." I said: "Doc, I don't think I will ever die by a Yankee bullet." He said, "You will get well."

I was taken, with a lot of others, to some nearby town or station and quartered. My first stop was in a small house. A few of us were put in a room, 16 or 18 feet square, and near to my right side was placed the 5th Texas color bearer. He was shot below the knee and through the fleshy part or calf of the leg. In camp near Richmond, after the seven days' fight, he spoke to me about taking the flag, and said there were some who wanted him for color bearer, but he cared nothing for the position, and asked me if I would accept it and remarked that he thought it would be in better hands with me. My words were, in effect, as follows: "You are mistaken, for I feel I am too cowardly for a flag-bearer to risk myself; and I find the oftener I can load and shoot the better able am I to maintain my honor. In fact, I have said I never would pick up a flag, going into battle, for I would not lay down my gun when I thought there was a chance to kill a Yankee." He took the flag and from what I saw and heard, he always bore it creditably.

Now, returning to our pallets: We were not long there before I heard him sighing and at times in a low tone, mourning. I asked him his troubles and he stated he was going to die, and went on with a statement of his lamentable condition, telling me of dear ones at home and he so far away; and that he would never see them again. After he got through, I rather made fun of him, and said if I had been wounded no worse than he, I would at least keep on through the fight, and after that I would have good excuse to get to the rear and have a good time, and he ought now to be looking out for some sweet girl to talk to. He said: "Oh, well; that is the way you look at it, but if I had been wounded as badly as you, I would have died on the battle field." The conversation dropped here, and I gave it but little thought; for my mind was on getting a furlough and the good time I was planning. After a good night's sleep, I felt considerably refreshed and was ready for breakfast, which was soon served. My "boy companion," as I will call him—for his age made him near such—told me that he had slept but little during the night; and from that, commenced talking of his lamentable condition as he had before. I let him talk at length and was satisfied that there was great seriousness on his part. I told him he must cheer up; that he was homesick and from what I heard, it took a determined will to throw it off, and that a man who could face shot and shell as he had, and at that, knowing he was the center target, had determination enough to not think and talk as he did, if he would try. We were that evening taken to other quarters, but separated. My parting feelings were pity and sympathy to see a dear boy like him suffering so much of mind. In a short time I heard he was dead, and I suppose the report was correct, as I have not heard of him since. The change of quarters was only an improvement in so far as the size of the room, as there were a greater number at one place. I remained at this place and had my two doses of morphine administered each twenty-four hours for quite a while. While there I had a severe case of flux* and I sure did suffer, as I was forced to lay on my back and the least motion of left hip caused great pain. While I was in this condition there were some of the boys discharged or furloughed. I well remember the parting words of two as they bid me good-bye: "Bill, we are sorry we will never see you again." My reply was: "I am not going to be off long, for I am only going to ask for sixty days' furlough." One of them remarked: "When you get it, it will be for the other world." My reply was: "Boys, if you don't get killed before, I will soon fool you by turning up in camp." Such talk as this had not a particle of effect on my mind. In due time the wound commenced cleaning and one-half of a horn pants button, half of wooden peg that I have mentioned, piece of drawers and pants, each the size of a silver quarter came out. From this, the wound healed rapidly. I was furnished water and cloth and did my own

* Bill's wound caused him to have an excessive discharge from the bowels.

wound dressing. In those days water and a wet cloth was what was mostly used for wounds; and with each wound I received, this was the only remedy, less acid, to stop gangrene in foot wound. When I left the hospital I had sixty days' furlough and a few months' pay. My transportation was by rail to the Mississippi River, and after crossing the river, walking. When about thirty miles out from Alexandria, Louisiana, I stopped one evening in front of a house steps, of what I took, from surroundings, as being the residence of a rich planter. There was a man on the front porch and I asked if he lived there. He replied that he was the proprietor. I asked if I could stay all night, and he answered that he did not take in soldiers. I told him where I was headed for, and that I was thoroughly worn out and could walk but little further without food and rest; and if I passed on I would not be able to make the next place, which would force me to lay down on the roadside. He still refused. I turned loose on him, and sure said enough, and from the language I used I guess that a man of his re-finement thought I was not well reared and had been keeping bad company. Among other things I told him that the war was not over yet and as I was in for the term it might fall to my lot to help keep the Yanks out of Louisiana; but I sure would quit fighting and try to get the other boys to do so when the Yanks turned his way, and that I would feel re-venged when I saw his place going up in smoke. He finally said: "I guess you can stop at the overseer's," and pointed to a house a short distance off. I said: "If he is a poor man, I can." I called at the house and was admitted without a word, and was treated first class. I told the overseer something of what I had said to his boss, but he said very little. By breakfast the overseer was advised of my condition and my mode of travel, which was walk a little and ride every chance when a

wagon was going my way. After breakfast he said he was going down the road a few miles and asked me to get into the buggy. I did so and soon saw a few miles stretching out. After traveling some time at a good gait we overhauled a wagon headed my way. The overseer seemed to have some authority over the colored driver for he halted him and instructed that he put me at the ferry landing, opposite Alexandria, which he did. I thanked my benefactor, and told him I guessed his boss was a better man than I thought he was, as I was crediting both of them for the ride and asked him to say to his boss for me that, should it fall to my lot to help keep the Yanks off of him, that I would do my best. Arriving at Alexandria, I was detained one day, waiting for the stage coach to leave. When it did, I boarded it, and was driven about forty miles. I alighted and walked about two miles to sister's.*
Some miles before I left the stage, seeing no one whom I knew and such a change after my six years' absence, gave me a feeling that I had never before experienced. Some times I would catch myself wishing that I had never come; for, after leaving my boyhood home, I had at times a great desire to visit it, as I had gotten it into my head that there was more pleasure in the surrounding country than any place on earth; and, in my case, I guess it was so; but now it seemed that all my pleasant anticipations were blasted. It did not prove so, however; for when I had accustomed myself to the change, the time flew fast. I remained as long as my sixty days' furlough would permit, making a fair estimate of time lost through detention in transportation, and I arrived at my command with three days to spare. I did not report for duty, thinking I would be more free to go and come at will.

* Bill went to the home of Mary Elizabeth (Mrs. Austin) Allen.

BATTLE OF FREDERICKSBURG, VIRGINIA

✦

I FOUND MY command just below Fredericksburg, Virginia, near the Rappahannock River. They were camped near the line of battle, on the brow of woodland hills. Soon after reaching the company, I got my gun and supply of cartridges, but saw little chance of getting off to train my gun. This I always did, when opportunity offered after getting gun and would test every few months. The enemy was strongly posted on the opposite side of the river, and were shelling the valley on our side. The next morning after reaching camp I went to the front. In passing along the outpost I met Captain Ike Turner of the 5th Regiment. He had quite a squad under his command doing outpost duty. He was on a public road that ran parallel with the river and was protected by a stone fence. His position was something over a quarter of a mile from the river—the country was open, both front and rear. He seemed to be glad to see me back and ready for duty, and said he had a job for me and that he was satisfied I could get the information wanted; said he had sent men to the front three times that morning, but all had failed. He said that it was thought that the enemy were putting in a pontoon bridge near a house on the bank of the river, which was directly in his front and from his view point, it was the only place of unseen observation, but the country was so open it was dangerous to approach, as the opposite banks were well elevated and lined with men and batteries, as I could see, and the men who had left hiding and attempted to crawl to the front had been driven back before they got far out. I looked to the front and left; saw some small timber growth, and said: "Captain, I guess there is a hollow or drain to the river and I will try that." His reply was: "It is some distance above the point and open to the house." I started and was but a short distance in the hollow when I found an old negro man and woman who were trying to get to the rear. The man was small in size, and his wife large and nearly helpless and if I remember right, she had one arm broken. I got what information I could and went forward. When I got opposite the house I saw, by crawling down the corn rows, that I would be reasonably safe in getting near the back of the house. The ridges ran in the right direction, therefore, I did not have to crawl over any of them to make my point. This movement was not on hand and knees, but on my stomach. When I was near and in the rear of the house, I crawled on my hands and knees and was soon in the house; found that it had been well bombarded, and from the looks of things, the occupants had moved hurriedly. There were a number of shots that had passed through the house and tore the inner contents in great shape. I picked up from the floor a good table knife and silver teaspoon. The house was on a desirable location near the river bank; it was of fair size and two stories high, and from inward appearances, had been occupied by wealthy people. I was soon on the second floor, but had to be very cautious, as the men with small arms and battery on the opposite bank were too close for comfort, and with the most of the windows broken out and several holes on the river side of the house, it made me crawl around on my stomach, in the wreckage. I made the lower corner of the room and took observation through a rent in the wall. I saw about three hundred yards below the house, the point of laying in the pontoon bridge, and the second bank at that point had allowed the material for the pontoon to be placed there at night and they could put it in unobserved by our lines during the day. I saw from the way the men were working that it was not a rush job. From the position in which I was I could see a large wheat straw pile below the house and about four hundred yards from the point of the pontoon landing, on our side. I was soon on my way out and made my report to Captain Turner, and asked if he objected to my spending the balance of the day on the straw pile, as I was much interested in the laying in of the pontoon. He said he had none; but it looked like great risk for individual gratification. I said there was no greater risk in making the hay pile than there was a mile off of river bank, as I had my way picked out and would get there unobserved, and that it was my judgment there would be no crossing till near dark, and I could run to the rear of the stack some distance and not be observed. I made my way back and was soon on top of the hay stack, sitting down. It was a fine place for watching the bridge gang, and was observable from our outpost. I thought the enemy would not attempt to dislodge me, for their only chance would have been to have gotten in the first shot and I was sure not to start it. I could have annoyed them greatly, had they fired on me and missed aim, for the straw heap was fully eight feet high and seventy-five feet long, and was too broad to be penetrated by cannon shot; and I guess their efforts to fire the house with its inflammable contents made it questionable as to the hay pile. I remained comfortable, sitting and lying, and sure did enjoy several hours of sight-seeing. The men looked at me considerably at first, but I was apparently unnoticed by the bridge gang, although the boys on the river bank who were in line seemed to be interested. I held my position till near dark, when the enemy commenced running over the bridge. I slid off the hay and made good time to the rear. Their crossing was a little earlier than I had expected, and as soon as they made the top of the bank, the bullets that came my way were many; but I made the run without any mishap. I have often thought since of the little judgment I used in not moving out as I had come in earlier. When I returned to camp, the boys were expecting battle the next day, as it was supposed they had all their pontoons in and would make the crossing that night. This proved true, and there was some lively times from that on, until the enemy crossed back. The Texas Brigade was held in reserve and was not called into action during the fight. After battling the greater part of the day, things quieted down for the night and all who could, went to rest. I had not been on my pallet long before I was ordered to report to General Robertson.* I reported and was ordered to the front to investigate and see if the enemy was not falling back. I soon was in front of our day's firing lines and saw that our men had protection by a railroad grade, and just to their front and some distance back the enemy's dead lay in great numbers. I passed on until I came near a closely deployed picket line;

---

* Brigadier General Jerome B. Robertson of Independence, Texas, was a veteran of the Texas revolution. He assumed command of the Texas Brigade when Hood was promoted to major general.

saw no opportunity of slipping through; could hear nothing to the front as the wind was blowing near a gale, so I slowly returned, pushing part of the time my left leg to the front or hopping; made my report and was ordered back to the company. My day and night's outing had nearly numbed my left hip and leg. A few hours' sleep rested it and I felt but little inconvenience from the wound after that. In the morning we were sent to the front to relieve the battle line that I had passed through during the night, and nearly all the dead Yankees who were in sight were naked. The enemy had recrossed the river and the position was too far from the enemy's line to permit of damage from field artillery, therefore there was but little firing done at Lee's right and the enemy's left; in fact, there was but little artillery practice heard, so when we had taken our place as relief, we were not confined to line and all who wished were sight-seeing a short distance to the front, as the dead bodies were all nearly naked and lying mostly on their backs. There was exposed to view a surprisingly large number of them who were so diseased, one would think: "Why weren't you fellows all in the hospital; or, were you run into our protected front to put an end to your miserable condition," and the idea that struck me was: "What will the Yanks be fighting us with next, and was not their ending the better for them." I think I saw the youngest boy laying beside what we took to be his father, that I ever saw, either dead or alive, on battle field. The condition of the dead bodies attracted quite a lot of sight-seers; so much so that it attracted the enemy's attention, far away to our right and up near the front of Fredericksburg, what was said to be five or six miles off, on an elevation, they had a thirty-two pound rifle cannon stationed and they turned it loose our way, and while they did our line no damage, they surely did some close shooting and put several shots near that tore good sized holes in the ground. As soon as they opened on us, we made back at quick time to lay down. While we were lying there, there was an amusing incident repeated several times in Company "F." There was one of the boys who was a natural coward, and when he was unknowingly caught in a trap he had no control over his fear. As we could see the puff up at each discharge of cannon, and the apparent long time it took for the shell to land, it was very trying on the nerves of the best, as they could feel that the shot was on its way and did not know what point of our line it was aimed at, which made every fellow for a few hundred yards in front have an indescribable feeling. The man referred to lay well flattened out with hat off his head, and held at arm's length to front, when the smoke was sighted and would stay in that position until the shot struck. After a few shots some of the boys seemed to get over the spell of fear and were making the best of a bad condition, and would call out, "Up goes smoke," which was often false. This poor frightened being would make an effort to bury his face in the ground, and strain his arms to the front to ward off the shot with hat, if it came his way. The act was so ridiculous that it was laughable, under the trying conditions, and the most of the company enjoyed the fun at the poor coward's expense. The enemy ceased firing when I suppose they thought we had learned to quit inspecting and enjoying their naked dead, as they could well see with their field glasses.

We were not kept in this position long, and while moving around I saw some parts of the battle line other than our front had been busy, for in front and near the city I saw more dead bodies of the right kind, covering broad acres, than it was ever my pleasure to see before or since. Those who have never battled often think such expressions as this are brutal. If they are correct, all courageous soldiers are brutes; for they enlist to battle, if so ordered, and as fighting is a dangerous thing, the more dead the less risk; and if one shudders at a dead enemy, he has but little place in the ranks, for it is a sure sign it is the other fellow's work. The faces of the dead on this field, and others, reminded me of the parting words of father, that: "They had the world to draw from." I saw that our part of the line had stripped the dead the most. The unacquainted would think that this work was done by the line soldier, but was not, only in case of actual necessity. It was largely done near Richmond and by those who made a business of it, as the clothing, when washed, was good stock in second hand stores and its benefit was that it supplied the wanting soldier and poor citizen at a low price. I heard of no effort to stop the practice, and there was no harm in stripping the dead, when the party stripped was a party to blockading our ports, which created the urgent necessity.

From Fredericksburg our movements were such that memory fails to connect my tramp for a while; therefore, I may fail to chain up as well as I have up to this time. If I remember correctly, we wintered on hills not a great way out from Rappahannock River and below Fredericksburg. At this camp I well remember my messes' experience with the winter house we built. The splitting of boards was rather hard, with the tools which we had, and as we had—with others—been instructed to build some sort of protection (as there was not a sufficient number of tents for all) my mess constructed our quarters by digging a pit about fourteen feet square and something over two feet deep, logging up sides so roof would be above our heads. The roof was made of poles with the necessary support underneath to permit a good amount of earth to be thrown on in cone shape to make a very warm roof, and supposed to be waterproof. We had not been occupying it long and had been praising our ability as constructors of warm quarters cheap, when one evening we had a heavy rain and did not have a leak. After the rain ceased, we visited a number of shacks and found the most of them reported "leaky." We went to bed that night with thought of warm and dry house, and were soon sound asleep. During the night we were awakened by dropping water and it increased to hard rain. We were up, striking lights and found the rain of the day before was just reaching us, as the rain had not run off but had gone into the roof. We moved bedding out before it was very wet and took to the open air for the balance of the night. The next morning we bailed our house out while the other fellows were having their laugh at our predicament; but before the next rain we had a tent fly stretched over the dirt roof and passed the balance of the winter comfortably.

As I was considered a good cook, the boys were always ready to fill my mess duties if I would cook. I was not stuck on cooking, and would only now and then do it out of regular time by helping in pastry part, and making light rolls; and as they were very fond of rolls for breakfast I generally got out of the mess wood gathering. While at this camp I made several rabbit hunts in the snow, but only captured two. The rabbits were plentiful, but the soldiers outnumbered them by great odds so that the supply was quickly exhausted. At this place, I guess the greatest snowball battle of the age was fought. It started near where we were quartered, by two companies, and they were reinforced from time to time, spreading from company to company, to regiment from regiment, to brigade from brigade, to division by opposing forces consolidating as they passed from one point to others; officers soon joined in, both line and mounted field, and somewhat brought about order. Couriers could be seen going to and from, same as in battle, with horses at speed, so the word was passed to the front and as there was one encampment after another charged, the excitement was grand; regiment after regiment, brigade after brigade and division after division joined in, until it was said the whole of Longstreet's corps had snow battled. When one tired he dropped out, and as I was one of the early participants, I did not see the ending; but it was reported that it ended about five miles from the place of beginning. All were defeated; all were victorious, as it were, with but two reported injured to mar the day's pleasure. There was an order issued prohibiting general snowballing. At this camp there was a vacancy in the company of lieutenant, and I was urged by some to run for same. I refused, with the same old story that I would not lay down my gun and soldier. I only served once as camp guard while in quarters. I was approached when relieved from duty by one of the company's officers and asked if I would accept a corporal position. I declined. He said the officers and privates thought I should not be called on to do camp duty. My reply was: "I have been in fighting line with the company in every battle when I was reported for duty, but I enjoyed getting in front when opportunity offered, and as yet had not failed to be at my post of duty at the time of battle and wished to continue as I had; for my chances, I thought, were good to have freedom of outposting now and then, and if I did accept, my position would be such that I would be with detail men when more than one was needed, and as it is, I select or am selected." In a short time I was told that I had been appointed corporal, so during the balance of the time I served with infantry I was never put on fatigue duty or camp guard. Neither did I ever serve as non-commissioned officer.*

We stayed long enough at this camp to closely forage the country for a good distance out; and the report was that there was not a fowl in that section, less guineas, and I guess the report was right; for there were two slick artists in my mess and there was a covey about a mile from our camp, and they tried often to capture one or more at night, but failed and finally gave it up and said the gun was the only thing that could capture a guinea; and as shooting was prohibited, the guinea was the only safe fowl in time of war. While at this camp in the valley near the right wing of our battle line of Fredericksburg, in a small house, I saw what I supposed to be the remains of the old negro man that I have previously mentioned helping his wife to the rear. When I saw the skeleton it was standing in one corner, stripped of clothing and the limbs were straight. From appearance one would suppose the man had starved to death. When I saw him alive he was under size and very lean. The skin of the corpse was dried and was brittle; and the roaches, from evidence of the number that were seen, had gnawed holes in the skin and eaten all the fleshy matter and by removing the skin one could well see the bones and muscles in place; and as I had some dread of foot or hand wound from seeing the suffering it caused, I at two different inspections closely scanned the foot and hand, and there is sure a net work hidden by the skin and flesh of the hand and foot. I have often thought what a valuable subject this would have been for a medical school.

---

* *Hood's Texas Brigade: A Compendium* shows on page 213 that Bill Fletcher was "Promoted to Sgt., Oct., 1863."

Leaving this camp, we did lots of marching but little fighting that I can call to memory. We finally struck the Potomac River at a point where it was said we marched out of Virginia, waded the river, passed through the corner of Maryland and into Pennsylvania the same day. The river was deep wading, so the lower part of man got a much needed bath. There were said to be two bands on the Maryland side, and from the continuous music I suppose there was relief, and they were there to cheer the weary soldier in his watery march. After crossing the river we marched a short distance and were ordered to stack arms and build fires and dry our clothing. It was said we were then in Pennsylvania. We soon had roaring fires scattered around of such material as was at hand, and as the enemy had educated us and it was the first time we were on what we termed "the enemy's soil." Fencing was good fuel when it was near at hand. While drying, it was reported that there had been several barrels of whiskey pressed, and we found such was the case, as the proper ones were soon passing around the drinks. I drank my portion to the dregs, and it was a bumper for me. A small percentage of the boys refused, and gave their share to others who wanted to repeat; so with empty stomachs, standing around the fire, it was soon showing its effects—some cutting antics, holloaing, or singing; and from appearances, the larger part fighting and parting combatants. One of "F" members, however, must have been enjoying the fighting as he grabbed up a stack of three guns and charged a near parting group. Just as he lunged forward he said: "G—— D—— you, let them fight." He struck an officer glancing, in the cheek, with the bayonet and made a slight wound, and I will state that was the first and last time I ever saw blood from the stick of a bayonet; except when a fellow was using it as a roasting fork in beef that was fat enough to bleed. One who reads this may feel curious to know what was done with Private Taylor. Answer: "Nothing." The bugle call to fall in line was sounded and we were quickly on the march. By this time my drink was having its effect and from the time it took it to wear off, it had given me opportunity to swear off several times. My whole desire was to lie on the roadside and sleep, but as we were in the enemy's country, I was fearful, should I drop out, I would wake up a captive; so I walked and staggered and my feelings were such that if I had been possessed of "Rockefeller's wealth" one would have been able to share it with me if he could have guaranteed safety from capture after I had slept off my drunk. I guess our officers learned a lesson, as they never after that offered drink. By the time we struck camp for the night, I was sobered up. We had been, before crossing the Potomac, well advised of the general order that there would be no straggling or foraging allowed while in the enemy's country. At the spring, where I went to fill my mess canteens, I saw the boys chasing chickens and nearby a house, said to be officers' headquarters, and from the horses, couriers, and such like, I credited the report. On returning to mess I told the boys of my find and I guess the order was intended for paper report, and not for soldiers. I said I would make a test if one other would go. All said: "I will," about the same time; but the one who got the tobacco and money from the peddler suited me best. By this time it was dark and there had been a strong camp guard thrown around us to keep us in. We left luggage with the mess and started, walked straight up to a guard and told him where we wanted to go, and that when we returned we would divide with him. We were soon out a mile or two and found a number on the same mission. We ran into two acquaintances and they joined us. The first place we stopped was the front steps of a residence, with three women sitting on the gallery. We made our wants known and were soon being treated royally. They seemed to have plenty of cooked food, as though they were looking for us. When we had satisfied our hunger, we moved on, each of the same mind that the women had furnished their share. We soon found a bee house that had lots of bee-hives in it, and from the amount of bees stirring in and about the place, we were satisfied that we were not the first. The question arose: How to get them. Some kind-hearted soldier heard us and said: "Rope them and run," and instructed where a rope was, near by. We soon had by great risk, the rope in place, and the word given to "run!" So we started in a sweeping trot, with men at one end of the rope and bee-hive at the other. We had to trot off some distance to get beyond hives that had been treated in like manner. When we stopped, we were soon at the gum, satisfying the inner man; but could take none to camp for want of a vessel. We did the fair thing, however, of returning the rope to its place.

We continued prowling around, looking for something to eat to take to camp. It was now getting well into the night, and walking near a barn we discovered a man leading a horse. We found he was taking the horse from hiding to feed him. He begged piteously for his horse, but we said we would be disobeying orders if we did not take it as it was a fine animal and just suited for cavalry. We compromised by him feeding the animal and going into the house and shutting up and not to be seen or heard. He soon had the horse in its stall and fastened up, as he had prepared its food. He well filled his agreement—we did ours and it was easily done, for we were not horse hunting.

We looked around and struck a milk house and soon had

our full of its contents. It sure was a night of feasting and there were no ill effects from our gormandizing. We then made a search for a hen house and found it some distance from the residence, and as we were not armed, we expected to run out of tights if pressed; therefore, we were very cautious and spoke in low tones at the hen house. The tobacco boy was soon in—making an examination, as I supposed from the time he was taking. We were near the hen house on watch, I was on the door side and had grown somewhat impatient. I said: "Why in the H—— ain't you killing and throwing them out?" Instantly there was a dull thump at the front door and it was repeated in quick time with several thumps. I stepped forward and felt and found some warm but lifeless large chickens. I remained squatting by the pile and at short intervals there would be another thump, and that went on for some time, and as I felt no small chickens, I said: "Enough large ones; want some frying size." So the thumps of less sound continued a sufficient length of time, to fill the order. I said: "Enough." He stepped out and the other boys were called and we gathered up the fowls and made some distance toward camp, struck water, had a drink and commenced to dress our chickens so we would make no sign taking them from mess hiding to cooking vessels. We soon found that we had an all night's job unfeathering our fryers and expended a good deal of strength to pluck one feather; and after trying them all we concluded that they were old bantams and left them. I have often wondered since if a bantam ever sheds its feathers.

We got back to camp, passed in as we had gone out, but our man was not at post to get his divide, as I suppose the officers thought it was time for thieves to be in bed and had relieved the guard. The next morning pard and I slept late, and when we were wakened for breakfast I got up and rubbed my eyes, which passed for washing. When I looked around I thought if general orders got in paper the ones who were out of that section might be gulled;* but our nearby neighbors could not help but think our superiors were not much obeyed. There seemed to be no hiding and from the amount of good food in sight, I asked if the last general order had been revoked while we were out. At an opportune time that day I asked my prowling chum if he would not put me on to how to get chickens at night like he did without noise, as he seemed so slick about it that there must be some sleight of hand work in it, or he had the power of making all near by deaf, as the other boys said they had heard nothing, same as I. I told him he was the best chicken getter in the mess and that the boys would kick more when he failed to do his part if it were not for this redeeming trait. He said: "Bill, I will tell you, but you must not give it away, as the other boys would make less failures and there are not enough of the chickens to go around; that the way most people stole chickens at night was not worth while walking far for, as they crawled up to a roost with plenty of chickens, and would lay their hands on one and let it flutter and hollow and then the balance would raise a great racket and leave their roost; dogs, if any, would be waked up and one was apt to run, thinking there would soon be a gun pointing his way. Be sure you don't tell." I promised again. "I caught on from an old negro, and it is done in this way, but will only work where chickens roost low, as most of them do and when one can reach from the ground or by standing on a box or barrel it is no trick at all to get all you want; but it will not work if you have to

* Bill used "gulled" synonymously with "cheated."

75

climb, as chickens seem to have a great dread for climbers and you cannot get up easy enough, as they will hear you and commence raising a racket. When you get under their roost, let the chickens get through with their low croaking, and stop operations—if they do hear something and start it again, wait till all is quiet and commence again. Put your hand on the roost (back up is best) move it along the roost until you touch a foot; the chicken will raise up; slip your hand under and when he puts his foot down on your hand, you will know about the size of the chicken and direction of its head. If you don't want the chicken, or its head is toward you, turn your hand and draw from under its foot and the chicken will put its foot back on the roost. If you want the fowl, change so your hand will be on other side of the roost. This will put its head from you. Repeat operation and when one foot is on your hand, slowly slip your hand to touch the other foot and it will raise and put that foot on your hand. When both feet are on your hand, raise a little, then when the chicken's body is clear of the roost, lower gently, at the same time swing across breast and raise left arm at the shoulder. When chicken's body is under, give quick up motion with chicken and downward clamp with your arm. As you are doing this, grab the neck with left hand, and with the other hand clamp its head, give a twist and pull and neck is broken. Hold for a moment—this hard squeezing and lack of freedom to flutter will quiet the nerve instantly. Holding by head, lower the chicken until ground is touched and turn loose. If on the floor, hold to the head till it touches the floor. This can be repeated as often as wished, and the darker the night the better, as the owner cannot peep through a crack and see you, and as he hears nothing he would at once leave, and if light is seen, one has time to creep away." I guess one would be less at ease now, for the electric snap light would be on his mind. He said "He guessed the reason why chickens jumped when their necks were broken or cut off was that they had too much freedom, and it took them longer to find out they were dead; but when squeezed and stretched so they could not move, they knew instantly they were a goner and it was no use kicking."

We were kept on the go and the most of the time were feeding well, with our camp guards out at night, who were taken in when all tired men should have been in bed. It was amusing, in passing through towns, to see the bevies of girls hanging over yard fences and the gabbing back and forth. They would some times ask what regiment or brigade was that and at the answer "Texas," there seemed to be the word "Law" well drawn out.

Battle of
Gettysburg,
Pennsylvania

IN THE COURSE of time we were thrown into line of battle near Gettysburg, and as our brigade ranks were well depleted, we did not make a very long battle line. We were said to be near our right; and in front, less than a mile off, the country looked well elevated and from barren spots I took it to be rocky. While laying in position one of Company A privates, and I think of Galveston, stepped to the front and started to offer prayer, something that I had never heard of in our part of the line under like conditions. He was ordered back into line and just then a bursting shell wounded three of his company. This happened only a few feet to my right, before going into battle. In times of battle there are generally what are called color companies. I suppose they are called so by their position in regimental line with colors and special color guard also. I was, on this occasion, color guard with a small detail with A. and F. color companies. The sergeant ordered me to colors. I protested, saying I was not the man and he had often heard me express myself. He said: "Go ahead." We were soon forward and near on the opposite side of the valley. We routed pickets and scaled rock fences, and worked our way to the front rapidly, with pickets giving away before us, firing but little. We soon struck the foot of the hill, and found it rough and rocky, with large boulders now and then, so our lines were not at all times well closed. We soon were near enough the enemy's line for them to open fire. We had but poor chance to retaliate with much effect. Our men near me commenced falling rapidly and especially color bearers—if I remember correctly, I saw the colors fall five times, the last time in the hands of the sergeant who had ordered me to act as color guard. In falling, the flag staff struck my head in front of my face. As it went down my forward motion caused my feet to become somewhat tangled. I gave a kick and said a curse word, and passed on. This happened near the end of our journey, and I know not who picked up the colors, but I have often thought: "Did the sergeant see all the color guards cut down; and thinking I was going to carry out my oft repeated declaration, pick it up in my stead?"

We stopped advancing, without orders as far as I was concerned, as I had heard none. Another man and I were well to the front, behind rock; the enemy was only a short distance up and so near over us that with good aim we could have near been shot in the top of the head, either standing or kneeling. At this point a field officer a-foot passed just to our rear and stopped a moment and looked up and said: "Boys, aim well." I said: "Cousins, move on; you are drawing the fire our way." He started with a determined look; and I thought, and think yet, that it was the bravest act I ever saw—a man inspecting a shattered battle line, with the enemy holding a position at such great odds leaning over their protection to shoot to hit our position. We did not attempt to scale the hill for it would have been a good job on some parts for one used to mountain climbing stripped for the business. This hill may be erroneously drawn, but it was well photographed on my memory as I have stated. We did not hold this position long before the order was passed on the line to "Fall back." I had no fear of the enemy charging and capturing the retreating forces, for they had ample dead and wounded to satisfy them, if all parts of our line were as badly butchered as at the point I went in and out. I learned some time afterward that the peak was called "Roundtop" or "Heights." Have never learned whether it was named before or after the battle. When we were in a scattered condition and had gotten out of danger and rather under the brow of the first elevation which we struck as we were going in, we were halted and lined and ordered in again. We advanced this time, knowing what was ahead of us if we went far, for the acts of the men soon showed that we were of one mind. We forwarded without a murmur, until we struck the danger point. The men about faced near as if ordered and marched back. The command "Halt!" was not heeded. Just as we wheeled I heard some fellow squeal for dear life. I looked and saw it was a lieutenant hopping, with a big toe shot off, and with his good sized and stout lungs he made more racket than I ever heard from one wounded man. We were stopped before we went far, and were about faced and ordered "Forward!" We made a few steps to the front and again without orders about faced and marched back to protection under the brow of a hill and were halted. There was quite a lot of censure for the last two forward movements by the men. We were held in position until dark and went forward on rising ground and put up a line of rock protection. When day dawned, we could see or hear little of our helpless wounded, the greater mass of them being well to the front and out of sight. We were not bothered by firing from the line as we were out of sight, but the enemy had few sharpshooters who were posted on the hillside that had favorable points of opening through timber, and when one would get a few yards to the front, before these openings, they would hurriedly get back. There was some attempt to dislodge the sharpshooters but failed. We lay in this position all night and most of the next day. To our left during the day there was a charge made by what was said to be Pickett's Division. From our elevated position we could see the battle line in the valley and hear the roar of cannon that were on an elevation to the rear. It was claimed that there were one hundred and forty cannon attempting to break or terrorize the enemy's line in front of Pickett's Division. There was sure noise enough, from the roar of guns and bursting of shells, to have moved the Yanks when the Rebs charged, if they had been movable; but they were like those in front of Hood—had a good thing and knew it, so the right of Lee's army had battled hard and met defeat at each attempt to turn the enemy's left. After all of this happening, as a participant the first day and partly in sight of the butchery the second day, was, as far as I was concerned, discouraging; and it looked as though our officers were blind, in so far as that part of the front was concerned. It looked to me that a flank move would have dislodged the enemy, or at least, battled near equal positions. While lying in the position, one felt reasonably safe, provided he kept behind rock piles so the sound of battle was plain enough to satisfy that there was but very little changing of position; and as we were the advancing army the reading of the different parts of the line added nothing to relieve one's mind who had been through the experience of the evening before and knowing just to our front lay the unfortunate Reb who was wounded and suffering. So, taking conditions as they were, I was at that time on the dark side of life's thoughts or, in other words, hope in a depressed condition. While behind the rock protection in the evening of the second day, word was passed along the line to get ready to charge the front. The order shocked me, and my feelings were indescribable; in fact, I had a bad case of cowardly horror. I felt sure if I retraced my steps of the evening before, it would be the ending of me. I could see no object in the move, only to sacrifice the extreme left to save the army on retreat, as I felt we had gotten a good whipping all along the line and I was considering which was preferable—disgrace or death, for I felt as one feels when fright and disgrace at one and the same time has possession. I tried to force manhood to the front, but fright would drive it back with a shudder. I was in this state of torture for at least fifteen minutes. I was laying behind rock protection and dropped asleep with fear and disgrace to be my portion. I had slept but a few minutes when our batteries behind opened fire on the enemy's supposed line, to confuse, and then we would be ordered to charge. The guns were not elevated enough and were doing fine work on our position. The bursting and flying pieces of shell and rock put us in a panic condition—we could not drop to the front and protect ourselves, for we would be exposed to the enemy. Our field officers just to our rear were dismounted and had great trouble to mount. They soon got a few mounted by giving help, and ran to the rear and stopped the firing. All was confusion, but we soon got back into line and orders countermanding the charge were passed down the line. When I awoke my fears had gone and when I heard the countermanding order I had a feeling of regret, thinking what a great relief we could be to our wounded by dropping our water canteen by their sides as we went forward; and possibly through some unforseen condition we might be able to remove them to the rear. I think my feeling about the necessity of aid was felt as much as those who needed it, and I have often thought: What is mind, and what causes its changes; for, in this instance when the order was received for the forward move, I at once was a transformed being; feeling all the pangs of horror that one could have flash over him, feeling as I once had great pride, knowing that I had done my duty under any and all conditions to the best of my ability, and now all was lost, if I did not go into the charge and be shot down to avoid disgrace; for I knew I had been as far to the front the day before as any one I could see to my right or left, and I well knew that the enemy had the night previous to arrange or strengthen their position, if such was needed; but this was not needed, for nature had long ages since done the work, and knowing the great disadvantage that was to our front caused the thought: "Where is our boasted Lee? Why is this ignorance?" As for Longstreet, he was excusable, as far as I was concerned; for I always thought he was on the wrong side for we had no men to spare in a bull dog fight, for even with victory we were the losers. He was kind and courageous and by nature was a fighter, but not a tactician, and when he was assigned near an impregnable position that was made so by nature, with an insufficiency of men and short time limit, what more could have been expected? In my opinion, if he was in the battle line as ordered, with instructions to force the front, there was none better capacitated to have made a success, if such was possible, with the means at hand. I have heard since the war some censure cast at General Longstreet for Lee's defeat at Gettysburg, but heard nothing of the kind from the battling soldier who was a participant in the great struggle. Records of his orders could be the only proof that would satisfy my mind that he was at fault—so I have always thought how cruel to idolize without a fault, and sweep errors aside and heap them on others. I will always censure some officer, but not knowing who, cannot specify to my satisfaction the individual blame. Why were we fighting an impregnable position—was it ignorance? I guess so. It was a very unfortunate condition for the right of an army with true and tried men being shot down like dogs.

We moved to the rear some distance, just as dark was near, and the enemy did not follow up closely. On our way to the rear, and a few hundred yards in front of where our men were halted and remained for the night and part of the next day, I was left at a rock pile and from what I could see the next morning, I was the extreme right outpost of infantry. My position was on the brow of an open elevation and narrow open valley in front, with woods on the opposite side. When I was left, and told that I would be relieved in due time, which time did not arrive, however, until the next day, when I was called in. When our line marched out I asked no questions, but supposed I was either forgotten or the place could not have been easily found; or would have put the relief, crawling in, subject to fire from foe or friend. The rock pile gave me protection, either lying down or sitting in a stooping position. I was not on the outpost long before the enemy, or at least dark objects were seen in front. I knew there was no stock at large, and if a Reb was there, he was out of place, so I challenged none and got in several shots during the night and my aim or report of my gun had the effect at least of moving the object. To my left some two hundred yards I would now and then hear gun reports, so I felt safe on the left, as in the twilight the enemy would hardly attempt crawling through. But to my right it was different, for I heard no shooting and during the night at two different times I let the man crawl well up on the elevation, about seventy-five yards to the right, before I notified him of his mistake. So I passed what seemed to be an unusually long night all alone, with eyes to the front, rear and flank. Fortunately, I was well supplied with tobacco and one who has never used it does not fully appreciate its comforting effects under similar conditions. When daylight came I could see my surroundings and the troops to the rear. I could easily be seen from our front, but saw no effort being made to relieve me. I had not unrolled blankets from my shoulder to keep off the cold morning air; therefore, being more confined as day approached caused a somewhat chilly sensation, but I dare not expose for exercise, for the Yanks on the opposite side of the valley in the woods did too close practice at the rock pile for comfort, whether they saw my head or not. As the day wore on, I got very sleepy and with all the force I could bring to bear, it was almost impossible to keep awake. I had heard of the use of tobacco amber or spit in similar cases, so I gave it a thorough test several times, used it liberally on my eyes, and it sure will keep one awake so long as the pain is greater than the desire to sleep; but I guess after a few applications, if one could see himself in a mirror, there would be a dirty pair of red eyes showing; so with burning eyes and a great desire to sleep, my lot was a hard one. As I have stated, I was in sight of our line, and one of my mess companions, a Beaumont boy by the name of Taylor,* got permission to relieve me, which he

---

* This was probably the William M. Taylor listed on page 216 of *Hood's Texas Brigade: A Compendium*. He was recruited at Liberty, Texas, on March 10, 1862.

did by crawling part of the way. A few shots near him as he crawled in did not deter him. When he reached me he said: "Bill, go to sleep. I have come to relieve you, and will call if the Yanks start to advance." I guess the sound of his voice had no more than ceased before I was sleeping. I slept nearly two hours, he said, when he awoke me and said they had called for us to come in; so we started in a stooping zig-zag run with a few bullets to enliven our efforts. When we reached the command it was in readiness to move, but before we did, there appeared to our right rear, quite a force of the enemy's cavalry. They were lined up about one-fourth of a mile away and had the appearance of forming for a charge. There were, a short distance to our rear, some residence buildings and they were soon burning to clear the rear which would have been front, if the charge had been made. The sight of a long line of mounted enemy and the roaring and hissing of the fire and a threatened front, made the position one of awe. Our cavalry soon put in their appearance and had a brush with the enemy's cavalry and they dropped out of sight.

While on the outpost during the night I could hear the rumbling of the enemy's artillery and wagon train going to our right. When we moved out and were marching to the rear, I was still sleepy, and at the first halt I was down on one side in the mud and getting the much needed sleep. I was told that I had caught up twenty minutes on lost sleep. When a person is in this condition, they are not very choice of pallets. I have seen men fall and not wake. I have curled up in the corner of a rail fence and slept more than once, to keep out of mud and water. I have often heard the remark "dead asleep," and in such an instance it is near a fact. When night came we were allowed to unsaddle, as it were, by stripping off our accoutrements and spreading blankets, if we had one. We continued this weary march for some days and stopped a short time near the Potomac River. Here I got to go to the rear as the enemy were following. I saw some of them skulking about three miles out. I got some rations and returned. We broke camp that evening after dark and started marching again. My shoes were old and so were my clothes. My pants were frazzled and split up to the knees, so I cut them off just below the knees, and thought if I looked like I felt, I was a fright. Short sleeves worn to near point of the elbow, no socks or drawers, and knee breeches. It was not long after leaving camp, marching in mud about six inches deep I lost the sole of one shoe. I jerked off the upper and tried walking a short distance with one bare foot. It looked like at nearly every step there was a rock to jam between toes as my foot slipped down and forward. I soon pulled off the other one, thinking that I could walk with less danger to both. This was a mistake, so I soon got out of the road and made my way as best I could through woods and fields, keeping near the road. I found that there was quite a lot of straggling, which was ordinarily done on the side of the road. I traveled all night, and by daylight my feet and legs were well bruised and torn by dewberry vines which always caused me to halt and back out. When day arrived I found I, with others, was in the rear of the infantry and just in front of our cavalry rear guard, the enemy's advance, which was cavalry, opened fire. I struck a trot, hurt or not, and by the rear guard fighting the most of the stragglers struck a pontoon bridge and soon were safely over the river. The stragglers numbered here had been so great as to wear a path and there were often miles of it that were soft and springy and not muddy. When a fellow struck a place of this kind he moved with but little or no pain. We struck camp some distance from where we crossed the river at, or near what I was told was Bunker Hill. We remained here several days, the most of the time sitting, or lying down, patching up. Here we were soon supplied with rations and the most needy—shoes and clothes. While here only a short time, one of "F" boys was prowling a short distance out and discovered several barrels of whiskey, hid under straw in an old house, some distance from a residence. He came to camp and told some of the boys in the company and they gathered up all the canteens of the company and filled them. It was soon noised around and whiskey was soon in the different nearby camps; and in some instances, the camp kettle was filled. There was soon, as far as I could see, drunken soldiers—it was said that half the camp was drunk and the other half doing the little camp duties and keeping the drunken ones straight. This went on for part of a day and night and most of the drunk sobered up. I guess that the sober ones had hidden the whiskey from them so the sober fellows had their drunk, and were cared for by the first crowd. This is the way the boys talked; but it was not quite so bad. My pallet mate had taken both days. There was a funny incident happened to him the second evening. He was one of the kind that could be full and not down. I called "Mc" to where I was lying and told him I was nearly dead for water, as I had drank none since he had filled my canteen. I started to pour the remaining whiskey out but he grabbed the canteen and said he would give it to some fellow, or empty it at the spring, and as he started, the boys who were lying around threw him their canteens, so he left with six or eight. He was slow in returning and I wanted water awfully bad, although I had not taken a drink of whiskey, as I yet remembered my vow on the first day in Pennsylvania. It was reported that

"Mc" was found nearly drowned in the spring and had been dragged out and the canteens were scattered around, so I up and started, regardless of sore feet, and found "Mc" on his back, sound asleep, with his purse on his breast and canteens nearby. I filled them, aroused "Mc" and put the canteens on his shoulder and he staggered back to camp. I asked what was his intention when he put the purse on his breast and he said: "To catch a damned thief."

After resting up at this camp we started on the move— with no enemy within hearing. While moving about there were two or three long range telescope guns received for division or corps—I don't remember which—and I was told by several that they knew I would get one; but I would answer by saying: "I guess not, for I would not accept one if offered, for I did not think they were a good brush gun or one that could be dragged around on a crawl." It was not long before Captain Ike Turner spoke to me in regard to long range guns, and said he had a say in the allotment and he guessed I would hear of his opposing alloting one to me and recommending "Dickey" and for fear I might feel hurt about it, he wished to explain. He said there was a move on foot to detach him from command and allow him to select his men and form a company of scouts, and knowing me as he did, I was one whom he had in mind as that class of soldiering suited me best, and that I could render services at the front that would be creditable. I thanked him and said: "Captain, you could not, in my opinion, put the gun in better hands than Dickey's; and I think he enjoys outpost sharpshooting, and as for nerve and aim, he has both—he may be a little short in caution, but it is better that than too cautious." Captain Turner—if I remember right, was subsequently killed near Suffolk, Virginia, while standing on top of the breastworks, therefore, I heard nothing more of the scouting company. While near Suffolk, I served twenty-four hours near and in front of the enemy's fortifications in a pit on a barren hill. In front of the breastworks there was a line of protection to retard a charge, if such was attempted. This was done with small trees which had been felled with tops pointing from works, with limbs cut back to sufficient stiffness and sharpened. The way I reached my pit was after dark, being deployed with others some distance to the rear, with instructions to cautiously go forward and when the man in front had come out and met me, he would point the direction and I would do the same when word was passed along the line of pits of relief next night. So when the man was out and at me, he pointed and gave about the distance and finished his remark by saying: "It is a hell of a place." I went forward, stooping low, and had no difficulty finding it. The pit was of sufficient size for me to kneel or sit down in. The dirt which had been taken out was thrown to the front, so when in a well raised kneeling position, one could well see an object on or in front of the fort. As I had not been in the "kneeling business" much I got awfully restless at times; but as there was a big fat corpse laying nearby that I had discovered, it was a gentle reminder—"keep quiet." During the night there were some bullets passing which was evidence that not all in the fort were sleeping. When daylight came I saw I was uncomfortably close, but safe to a great extent, with proper caution. The enemy did their firing through holes and one could only tell when a head was there by the smoke, as I could not see through the hole. Suppose the rear was darkened to prevent seeing, but the distance was such that when one raised his head on seeing smoke, by quick action it would be out of harm as a bullet whizzed over. So our only target was port holes and the enemy's—our raised heads. I improved my shooting chances somewhat during the day by putting hat on end of ramrod and exposing crown to sight dodging it down when bullet whizzed by. I followed this up at intervals without shooting and when the boys would get tired of shooting my way with no apparent effect, they would direct their efforts to other pits, and probably the pit man was practicing a similar game. By this means there was a good deal of firing from the fort with very little on our side; but when the boys would find the enemy lagging they would soon start them by shooting at holes. The words, "Fall back," were passed the early part of the night and as one had nearly grown in a crooked condition, it did not bother him much to stoop low. When reaching relief the direction was pointed and finished up in about the same way as my instructor. When I reached camp several of the boys told me they were going to take a certain man out and whip him. This was the man who had fortified with his hat at Fredericksburg. They said he had such a horror of the pits, that they told him his turn was coming soon, and he had made a proposition that he would go out from camp and strip and they could get switches and whip him as much as they wanted—if they kept him, in someway, off of pit duty—and they would have been through with the job by then, but were waiting so I could see the fun. I soon persuaded them to desist, as it would be a brutal act and they would regret it to such an extent that they would suffer more than the subject, as his punishment would only be momentary, compared with their regret, and that I would see the next day if I could not get him detailed to wagon train. The man seemed to be resourceful and had well greased his shoes during the day, and from what I was told had made the job rather public; so the next morning, when he turned out his shoes were gone. There was a searching and inquiring for shoes but they could not be found. Some one asked him who he supposed had them, and he said he guessed a dog. Then some one of the boys who had seen him grease them, said: "I guess that's what made you grease them so much yesterday." The boys caught on and quit hunting. I went to the company's commanding officer and asked him to send him to a wagon train as I thought he would give good service there to hold his job, and that I had on several occasions heard him express a desire to be there as he could not fight; and it was a fact, as we all knew. The officer assented. Then I asked him to have him out of the camp before night, for it had been said to me that if I had not put in my chops he would have had good excuse to keep out of the pit and would not have had to hide his shoes, so it was not long before a detail for duty at the wagon train was in his possession. The boys said: "That means ready for duty, and you had better put on your shoes before starting; for the wagon may be on the move before you get there." So he went a short distance and unearthed his shoes, put them on and started. On leaving, he said: "Good-bye, boys." One of the boys said: "Don't divide thanks with God: they all belong to Bill."

While at this camp I got tired, as usual, and applied for leave of absence to the enemy's rear and flank, with permission to select two men for companions. In a few hours it was granted, so I spoke to two of the company's boys whom I knew could stand hard usage and it would make their eyes glitter before I would get through telling them to get ready. I told them to take no grub, for we would soon be where there was plenty. We were off like a shot, and by a circuitous route we were soon well in the rear of the enemy's right. We pushed on, either by night or day, until we could see the battleships riding the waves at anchor. There were quite a number of them and some of them were not far out from our point of observation. We took it all in, so far as sight was concerned, and commenced retracing our steps. We were not sighted by the enemy at any time and only made near approaches to see the gunboats passing up and down stream. We were not molested in any way and found plenty to eat. Being several miles on the return, I started one of the boys to report, telling him I would somewhat change course, taking it leisurely coming out, and he need not return. I found about a day after he left that the enemy was moving and we were cut off, so we moved in sight behind them for a few miles and I was satisfied it was a flank move on our left, so we mended our pace, moving to our right and front to get ahead of them. While doing this, I discovered a lone man and soon satisfied myself that he was a "Reb." We hurried to intercept. When nearing him I saw it was our chum, and we made our appearance from hiding. His words were: "I was not looking for Yankees and knew if you fellows were anywhere around you would sight me in some opening." He had orders for us to return and find command on move, and to look out, for the enemy were moving. The first favorable woods we struck, I said: "Halt," and told the order bearer to lie down and sleep. He said: "You need not stop on my account." I asked if he had had any sleep since he left, and he replied: "No, but I am not tired or sleepy and will let you know when I feel the necessity." By hurried march and passing near the enemy's right we were soon in front and traveling in the supposed direction of our command; stopped to rest and sleep and not yet a murmur from our man. I said to him: "You are a remarkable man to travel the distance you have without sleep and not a murmur have I heard." He replied: "Bill, you did not take me for a spring chicken when you told me to get ready."

We struck our command the next day and in course of time were near Petersburg, camping in the woods. One night there came up a storm. The wind blew hard; the lightning flashed and the thunder roared. Men were up and crouched near and behind trees for protection from flying timber. It was soon over, however, fires were built, bedding and wet clothes warmed and we were soon asleep. The next morning there were reported two injured. We were moved from this point nearby to a place of more safety, where the timber was not so tall. It was near a railroad, the passenger train would pass this point at good speed. Just before the train was due, there would be seen quite a lot of men lined up on the opposite side of the track from camp. They seemed to be well organized, and there were to be seen numbers of small bushy saplings scattered near the track for quite a distance. Just as the train was approaching, the windows would be full, looking ahead, as is usual when one is looking ahead and something unusual is in sight, all of one accord seem to know it, and the most of them push well out to see. Just at the opportune time—up went brush and off dropped the headwear of the passengers—then the scramble for the booty commenced. This practice was soon discovered and a guard placed to prevent, but from change in head-covering in camp, this trick had worked well.

If I remember right, it was spring time when we were at this camp; and there was more poor beef issued, by odds, than ever distributed in the same length of time, to my knowledge. The public road ran near and along front of the camp and when the cow brutes were passing to the slaughter pen beyond, it was a common remark that we would draw beef tomorrow as the quartermaster was driving to see what to kill first—as all that could not travel were said to be for next slaughter. This was not a fact, however, but so near the true condition that it would be hard to draw the line, as I would see the herds passing the road and visiting the slaughter pens, from sight, the conclusion I reached was as follows: The beef stock of all ages and sizes was exhausted in that section, and that we were gathering in the milch cows and one would think, "Old lady—your time next, and if your destiny is a flight to the great unknown, what a meeting of the herd of mother, children and great, great-grandchildren; and if death could be reached by desire, that you certainly were not a resourceful brute." In every brute there was depicted the wanting condition of the owner. The once pride of the family was slowly but surely starving to death and the end was near, for there were numbers that one would think when they lay down that they never would rise again until skinned and carted away to their last resting place—the soldier's stomach. The most of this meat, when cooked, would turn to jelly and one would think of sweetening. It was not necessary to have a peg to hang it on—throw it against a tree and it would stick. Need not necessarily be a nearby tree, as there was but little danger of its being stolen, as each fellow had enough of the kind. After being thrown against the tree it had the appearance of some hideous picture of a sea monster trying to climb down, as the tendons would stick where they came in contact with the tree and would slowly stretch from the weight of body whether the entire piece would go to strings, or not. We never made a test, but I have often pulled meat off—if such it could be called—when the meat was from two to four inches below where it first struck. If the reader of this undertakes to make test to prove the correctness of this statement, I would ask him to go for his material where he can get fair samples under like conditions. Here was where it was reported that some men ate the unborn calf if it was spotted. This word "spotted" was to denote one that had the hair on.

BATTLE OF
CHICKAMAUGA

‡〓‡

FROM THIS POINT I will take the reader to Chickamauga. It was reported that Longstreet's corps was reinforcing
Johnson. When we left the train we were marched a few miles
and thrown in line of battle and forward no great distance
until we were near the enemy and were ordered to lie down.
While lying here, to our right the battle was raging and a few
bullets being sent from our front that were coming uncomfortably close, under the nervous strain. I fell asleep as I had
often done before, under like conditions, and there was, from
what I could learn, a small percentage who would take the
same. Sleep always has a quieting effect, if only for a few
minutes, and I have often remarked that if a fellow wanted a
fight out of me, I would advise him not to wake me up to
get it, for I would be cocked and primed for the fray. I was
shaken and ordered to rise, for just then the enemy raised a
yell and charged, throwing a hail of bullets our way. We were
ordered to charge, so we plunged forward with a yell, firing
as we went. When near, the enemy broke and with but little
effort at returning fire, so things were going fast our way. A

short distance to the enemy's rear where they started the charge, was a high well-built worm rail fence, and as I suppose it was the least of their thoughts of having to return that way, or they would have had it torn down to clear their rear. At this point we were crowding them so close that they had no time to push down the fence or to climb it. My position in line put the corner of the fence about fifty yards to the left in passing to the front and about sixty yards from the corner stood a house about ten feet from the fence; and on the opposite end of the house was a dirt chimney. This I would pass near, going to the front. The enemy who were to my front and right were running over a hundred yards off. A great number of the enemy who were running down the fence and turning the corner attracted my attention from my immediate front. Between the house and fence there was a block that extended nearly back to the corner of the fence—a great majority of them were in a pushing motion and jammed and at close range. I got two shots and thought—oh, for a shotgun loaded with buck shot! I saw I could not get loaded in time to get a third shot before the jamb would be broken, so I struck a long trot and was loading to get a shot just as I would clear the far corner of the house. I was passing the end of the house about twenty feet to my left when something struck my left foot as I had it up and thrown forward. As I came down on it I fell forward, striking the edge of the hole that was made in removing dirt for the chimney; so in rolling into the hole I landed on my back, stretched full length. Instantly I saw I was well protected, and from sounds, I supposed a piece of flying shell had hit hard enough to trip me. There had been no pain up to this time, so the idea struck me that I was not wounded and had a coward's position, and I was liable to be seen in it. I raised my head to get up, and as I cast my eyes to my feet, I saw the leather on the left shoe torn near center on inside. I turned my foot and saw rent on the outside near the heel. I quickly removed the shoe and found I had a bad foot wound made by a bullet. The hole, when lying down, was all one could wish to protect; but fear of capture put me at once hopping. As I was passing back about seventy-five yards, I was near an oak tree about twenty inches in diameter; there was a wounded Yank sitting down, leaning against it. This gave him protection from the bullets of his own men. Pain here struck me and I felt faint, so with a hop or two I was at the Yank's side, and as there was not room enough for two, I gave him a shove, saying: "The day is ours." He fell over in a doubled position on his side, made no attempt to move, but was groaning. I was not more than well seated with back resting against the tree, when the sound of volley firing rang out and bullets flying thick, and the Texas yell raised. I knew our boys were charging reserve. I instantly threw myself far enough around the tree to see the front. There were our boys charging in scattered battle line and the enemy firing from solid column. I knew the enemy were doing but little harm as their bullets were flying high, but I thought discretion was the better part of valor and that I would hop on; so I started and would become blind and fall about every hundred feet, but had no more than hit the ground full length before I was scrambling up and off. This falling continued for some distance, but all the time I had an eye for a dead Yankee to prowl; so I soon was near one and stopped, kneeling and went through him, as it was called. He was a poor corpse and it was a poor haul—his knapsack was good but was light and as I did not have time to make an honorable exchange, I had it off and on my shoulders, over mine, in quick time. I picked up a gun and tried to use as a crutch, but soon dropped it, as I found I could make faster time hopping and speed was what I was after. I struck a "hide-out" and he offered help. I told him he should be at the front; that I was making good time. He said he was going no further, and I said: "You can help me then, and in that way be doing something for your country." He was quickly by my side and I was resting my hand on his shoulder but saw it retarded my speed. I became blinded and fell. He helped me up, asking if I was shot again. I replied: "No, and will not need your services." Our reserve was standing just in front. He pushed on through, a few yards ahead of me; was asked how the front was, and replied that they were killing lots of our men. As I came up, they opened ranks and let me through, asking me how the front was. I replied: "We are giving them hell, boys." There was a chorus of voices: "He has been there, you bet," and such like. A few hundred yards to the rear of the reserve I found an ambulance. This was my second wound and I never got aid from litter bearers and only saw the two mentioned at Manassas, so I guess I always got out early in the game. At an opportune time I examined my knapsack, found several well written sweet letters and from the wording, that fellow sure had some sweet girl stuck on him for she was anticipating a happy meeting and ful-fillment of vows, when the "Rebs" were whipped and the cruel war was over. Letters did not arouse any sympathy in me, nor have I felt one pang of regret for being a party to breaking up that match. She wanted me whipped—she got that; I wanted dead Yankees—I got that. So both at least got part of their wants satisfied.

When I arrived at the field infirmary it was dark and there was straw for bedding. I was put in about fifty feet from operating table, with a few others between me and it. I lay there all night, bleeding slowly, as my wound was not of a nature that required immediate attention. Near the table, but not in line, was a stout young man who was shot through the head. From the sides the brain could be seen oozing out. He seemed to be suffering greatly and would rise, make a step or two, and fall. He repeated this time and time again for quite a while after day light. I don't know at what hour he was brought in, but I thought how brutal human custom was in this particular, and wondered if it was handed down from barbarism and why it was that doctor or friend could not end one's misery, even if done with the best method at hand and that was only a rock or club. With brutes we sympathize and aid—with man we do not, for death is the only relief. I have often heard the remark: "Poor fellow; he had better ten thousand times be dead." I look upon it as cowardice in time of great need, for true friendship is he who comes in when the world goes out.

During the night there had been a great number of wounded brought to this point. The doctors looked worn. You would often hear at such times that they drank too much, but it must take a good nerve to stand it and the best remedy to prevent breaking down to go through, as I have seen it, the long hours that their duty calls. Some say that it is not necessary, or other preventatives would do as well. When such remarks are heard by me, I say, "your opinion is not worthy of weight, as you have not been tried." As I lay on my pallet that morning and heard the continuous roar of battle to the front, I gave the different parts of the line the closest attention from the rifle roar. If I detected the least change in sound on any part of the line it was figured as far as my reason could in shaping the lay of the line of battle, and as the roar went on at times I would mark out in mind some quick change, some parts apparently at a standstill. At one time I had our left center giving, and remarked that if it did not stop soon I would start for the depot, which was several miles off. One of the "F" boys standing near, said: "Bill, how foolish; you would drop on the wayside long before you reached the point." My reply was: "I can hop as fast as I can walk, and it does not tire me much more than walking." Finally there was a perceptible decrease of sound on the entire line, and I felt much relieved. Slowly but surely our whole line was moving to the front and it was only a short time before one could not picture the shape of the battle line as the distance was so great that there was no distinction in the roar. One of "F" boys had received a shot in the side of his face and through the nose and was passing through, seeing what there was to be seen. He looked so disfigured by the shot and swelling that he looked funny. When he saw me he came nearer and we each explained the nature of our wounds and about the point we had received them. I then commenced joking him, telling him he would make better success courting when he got back, with his back to the girls. When I got through, he said: "That will be better than you; as you can't turn any way to hide your wooden leg." I said: "Yes, if I had one." I was debating in my mind on what the doctors would decide when I went on the operating table and was chloroformed for probing examination, so his joke struck me in a tender point that was hurting before he spoke. He said: "Don't you see that man up there (calling his name) he will come first, and you watch and see what they will do for him, for when I was at the table, Doctor Roberts (who was the regiment surgeon) told me that from what he could see, passing, the man mentioned and you would lose a foot." By this time I was well worked up and said: "You are a D—— L——, Frank." He said:

"Bill, watch," and walked on. His words sounded as one talking badly through his nose, and were laughable—when one was in humor for it. So I lay and watched. The man mentioned was soon on the table, examined, and foot cast in scrap heap. Just before operation was complete, or rather the binding was complete, Dr. Roberts* started my way. He halted when at my feet, and said: "Fletcher, I want to examine your wound," and in a stooping position, had partly got his finger in the wound, before I realized what his mode of examination would be. Under the pain caused and the impulse of the moment, my right foot was quickly against his left shoulder, and as his head was toward me, with a quick shove, I sent him backwards, but not hard enough but what he could keep from falling. His face was flushed when he steadied himself, and he said: "I will leave you alone, without treatment." My reply was: "Doc, that is what I want, and the fellow that I considered most to blame would make the mistake of his life if treated without my sanction, as that man (calling his name) has been treated—put under influence of something and when he comes to, his foot gone." That evening I was hauled to the station and put aboard car and was off, not knowing where. Was taken off to Augusta, Georgia, and I thought the doctor had sent me to the limit of distance. I was quartered in a good size church, bunked in a pew, with space filled in. I lay there with my head to the wall and feet to the aisle so my wound was convenient to dress, which was once in twenty-four hours. I attended to wetting cloth from time to time. The most of the dressing was done by Sisters of Char-

* *Hood's Texas Brigade: A Compendium*, page 216, lists "A. B. Roberts . . . Detailed as ward master at hosp. in Newman, Ga., Oct., 1863. Deserted in East Tenn., Mar. 5, 1864."

ity—it was my first experience and I was in love with the women and the uniform at once and have not gotten over it yet; for there is a feeling of gratitude uppermost when and where my eyes behold them. I have often thought: was that branch of the human family, as it were, the mother of the Red Cross Society. My early education, but I am proud to say not at home, however, was far different. It came from the Methodist and Baptist pulpits, as they were the only denominations that I had heard preach, and I was reared under their influence until seventeen years old. Nearly all of the old grandmothers, both white and black, caught on and there was no place in heaven for a catholic; but my opinion changed, after falling in love and my religious efforts ceased feeling: "If there was a God he was a just one," and if He in justice consigned the sisters to hell, there was no use of me trying, as I had already done enough to be on the unpardonable list. I am thankful, however, expressions have changed, if opinion has not, for the old soldiers would have been scrapping to this day. Don't discredit me, however, as throwing discredit at the people of Augusta, as one could not be more fortunate than to be allotted as I and quite a number were, but the sisters were on to their job and were thrown more in a motherly contact with the boys when the most of them were pining for a mother's or sister's care. I was soon furnished with a strip of bandage by a sister, long enough to swing my foot to the shoulder and I sure did play the act of expert hopper in town, as I was free to go and come at will; and distance had no terror for me. I would nearly every day take a long jaunt through different parts of the town trying, however, daily to get a pair of crutches. I made repeated applications at the hospital and shop, but it was some time before I obtained a pair. The shop men got to telling me that I was at the bottom of the list. I attracted some attention on my hopping rounds, and was often remarked about. The crutches finally came and I was proud of them—not as I was tired, but wanted a change. Gangrene had started among the wounded and there was an appeal notice published asking the citizens to take care of all the wounded possible, as it was contagious. A Mrs. McKinnon called in a buggy for one. I was hustled in and my treatment at the McKinnon home was royal; but it was of short duration. Gangrene in a few days set in where the bullet entered and I was returned to the hospital for treatment. Here they burned the wound with acid and it was very painful. The first three applications nearly gave me the horrors and especially the first. If I had been a drunkard I would probably have thought I at least was threatened with delirium tremens, as the worm or snakey feeling would start at the mouth of wound and make a hurried zigzag run up near the knee, then would return as though backing out, and running out of the wound. The relief was instantaneous when the sensation had passed out, but was repeated at short intervals for two hours for the first time, the others of less duration. By the time it was through, I was nearly exhausted. This treatment, if I remember correctly, was kept up for seven days, burning each day. After the distressing muscular sensation had passed off, the mind dread was well rooted and all the unfortunates would look forward to the coming day with dread. The hospital medical attendants through their ignorance, caused untold suffering. I suppose the disease was new to them. There finally arrived a doctor who was said to be a hospital inspector. He stopped the burning treatment and had warm poultice applied. Soon after the poultice application there was a great expression of relief and joy, both by patient and nurse. In a few days the wounds had sloughed and were healing nicely. My foot was gradually straightening or turning down, which would have caused me to walk on my toes. This had gone so far that the doctors who examined it left it to me, saying they would break it if I wished, but advised against it, as I would not have one chance in ten of saving it. I said I would prefer life with a crooked leg and walking on toes, to an artificial foot; so they said they would consider it no more. Near the front of the hospital, in the center of the street, was a public well where I would go in the morning to wash my face. I would jump up on the pump platform, which was about eighteen inches high, lean my crutch against the pump barrel and rest my knee on it to steady myself, make a few strokes and wash as water was running out of the spout. The Catholic church was only a short distance from the pump, on the same side of the street as the hospital. There was some order of service of unusual attendance one morning, and while I was washing there were a number of women and girls who came pouring out at the front entrance. I knew there would be quite a lot pass my way, so I was in a hurry to get through before they commenced passing. My knee slipped down the crutch until my toes touched the floor. The pain was sharp and from some cause I fell forward and heard the tearing loose or breaking at or near my ankle. I rolled off the platform in the dust, but was up instantly with crutches under my arm making fast time for the hospital, struck my bunk and sent a fast runner for doctors. They responded promptly, made an examination and said I had done what they were afraid to do, but would do their best to save my foot. The pain was intense. In about forty-eight hours the doctors reported it safe and instructed working ankle joint and pressing it back often, hurt or no hurt, and when it got well I would have a serviceable foot. I followed instructions, and came out all O.K.

Soon I was transferred some distance, with others, to a small town and remained there until I reported for duty. This place fed different from the Augusta hospital. They had the table set and the food allowance at each place. So, near meal time there was quite a crowd jammed against and near the dining room door, and when the door was opened, there was a scramble and rush to get the best place. The best place was the one the fellow thought as he passed the side of the table that had the most grub at it; but it was like picking apples out of an assorted pile. Men in our condition were generally hoggish, so there was quite a murmur of complaint about being half fed, and I was one of the chronic grumblers, as I could not see how we could get able for duty, being half fed. One day I was crutching it out in town and seeing a pair of scales in a store, the idea struck me to weigh. I went in, asked permission to weigh and was granted; so I hopped on the platform, leaned my crutch against the scale and tipped the beam at one hundred and eighty-two pounds. I tried weights back and forth on beam and found that they were in working order. The storeman was watching nearby. I asked him if the scales were right and he replied: "Yes." I asked for both buyer and seller. He said: "Why do you ask?" Answer: "Because I weigh one hundred and eighty-two pounds and I am not getting half fed at the hospital—and one hundred and sixty-five pounds is the most I ever weighed, well fed." He laughed heartily, and said: "Young man, it is not the amount of food you eat that you do best on. It is on natural requirements. Appetite is often greedy and should be guarded." I thanked him and returned to the hospital, thinking he had read

O. S. Fowler's* books. I told the boys in my room my experience, and said: "Boys, let's quit grumbling for I guess these fellows are on to their job and are fattening us up so we will be able to live a while by sucking our paw, when they return us for duty."

Leaving the hospital, I struck my command quartered in East Tennessee. The boys were faring very well and said when they struck the place there was lots to eat for both man and beast, but foraging was now getting some distance off and the country was nearly all Union people, and there was but little mercy shown; and a fellow had to watch the jayhawkers or he would lose his scalp, and now foraging was done by details of good number, as the jayhawkers were bad. I have often heard A. N. Vaughn relate some of his experiences while out trying to capture jayhawkers at night. They had surrounded a house of a noted one and burst open the door. They found him under a bed and with cocked guns pointing, the wife yelled out saying all the rough, abusive words at her command and that if they were going to shoot him, to take him from under the bed and out of the house, and to leave her no nasty mess to clean up.

At this camp I made application for transfer to the 8th Texas Cavalry, commonly called Terry's Texas Rangers. The examining board was slow reporting on me, or at least company officers had kept mum if it had been made, and others who had been examined had heard of their case, so I went to the company officer and asked why the report in my case was withheld. He said he would see about it, but tried to dissuade me from transferring. My reply was: "I think I know

---

* Osburn Squire Fowler was a popular writer of the mid-nineteenth century. He wrote and lectured on phrenology, physiology, and sexuality.

my condition best as I can yet do honorable and good service as a cavalryman." I would not accept mounted courier position, as suggested, as that was fighting without a gun; and to try further infantry duty, I protested, as my hip wound had nearly disabled me at times and I had pained and not murmured and I thought with the two wounds I would be a burden as six months had now passed and I could not walk ten miles; and as warm weather was near at hand the army soon would be moving, and I could not start in with a hard foot. This would necessitate my lagging behind with the wagon train and being called wagon dog, and the cavalry boys singing to us when passing. I thought I would prefer desertion, and desertion with me would have meant the passing of life with the unknown with a changed name. The infantry were good at guying the cavalry and thought the boys had little to do but to find Yankees for them to fight, and as the Yankees were so plentiful, they had an easy job. The cavalry boys vented their feelings mostly at the wagon dog when passing the wagon train by singing a song that was said to have been composed by one of the Terry boys, which ran as follows:

"Come, all you wagon dogs, rejoice—
      I will sing you a song,
If you'll join in the chorus—bow wow wow;
      When we go to leave this world,
      We will go above with sheets unfurled—
      bow wow-wow."

The term "wagon dog" meant the unfortunate on marches or those who were not able to keep up; and it made no difference how honorable a soldier was, he was subject to slurs and it was caused by the company he was thrown with, who were a few who played sick and in the most cases were ingenious cusses in their mode of deception. So, with the probabilities at times of being a wagon dog and my set determination not to be liable, in a few days after talking to the officer, I received a transfer to Company E 8th Texas Cavalry. I bought for a few dollars a horse and saddle which one of the infantry boys had. The horse was hardly fit for cavalry but would swap well when the trading conditions were right; but my mount was quite an improvement and relief to a tender foot. In my cavalry experience I soon found it was no soft job and its only catchy part was that it moved oftener and faster than infantry; and I felt when applying for transfer that if I remained with the infantry I would be confined to the camp, or in other words, would be at all times with the main body. While I expected nothing more in cavalry, yet I knew the changing and outings of a cavalryman were greater. I also well knew, or at least such was my feelings, that the rangers were well fixed with scouting material that were expert shots and horsemen, and that being the case fully satisfied me with my lot as cavalryman.

I enlisted in infantry, August, 1861, and was transferred to cavalry, March, 1864. There were a few others of the 5th Infantry who were transferred and all reported the same day. We arrived late in the evening. I looked up John Pipkin, a Beaumont boy, found he was just in from a near all-day foraging trip. The country was almost destitute of all food and living, less women and children. John divided his day's pillage with me and two other boys who were with me. John was of the kind that never went wanting if the other boys had it and the other fellow would not protest, for he knew John was liberal to a fault and would give away his last—let it be to-bacco, man or horse food, if the other fellow needed it. John said: "This dividing necessitates foraging tomorrow, and as we have to go a considerable distance, we will start early and I will take you to a place where I tried to get corn, but could not as the corn is in a house, under one post-corner bedstead and shucked, but guarded with an axe in the hands of the gamest woman I ever tried to deal with. She would neither sell for Confed., give, or allow a fellow a chance to steal." In due time we were on top of a hill about half a mile off and in sight of the house—up went smoke. John said: "She sees us and is notifying the surroundings, but there is no danger getting bushwhacked in a country like this unless you are alone, but squads are often shot at up in the mountains." We were soon at the house and dismounted and started to go in the door—the house was a log-pen, about fourteen feet square, puncheon floor, and large fire place at the end and door at the side—there stood the determined woman, with club-axe near. There was about a five gallon pot hanging over the fire full of water and it was boiling. She had in one hand the longest handled gourd I think I ever saw. The bowl of the gourd would hold about a quart. With one hand on the door-facing, and the stretch of both arms and the length of the handle she could easily dip water and when we ventured near she would give us a dousing. We had on caped overcoats with cape thrown over our heads; so, by turning our backs we would not be scalded. If a fellow turned quickly after the water was thrown, thinking he could rush on her and grab her, he would see his mistake, as she would, by quick motion, have gourd in the pot, handle in reach and axe in hand. We saw there were no words to persuade and no thought on our part of forcing, so other methods were resorted to by means of a lever to part the puncheon under the bed so the corn could be pulled out. She caught on, however, when the first man who had left the front returned and the second one went around the house out of sight. As the horses were standing not far from that end of the house, she could not see them, standing in the door; the second man had time to get a sack and was squatted down filling it with corn, when without warning, she sprang forward from the door with axe in hand at the mob in front. We were standing at a safe distance, however, and soon had a greater margin. As she jumped, we yelled "Look out," and it was well we did, as her play was to shoo us and get in her work on the fellow who was loading up sack. He was up and out of the way in time. She stood us at bay only a short while after this, seeing it was a hard job to guard both sides; so she proposed to let us in to get corn, provided we would promise not to be greedy. This we did and carried it out, but the first party filling a sack had discovered bacon under the house and had a piece in his sack; so we caught on and two others did likewise, without detection. The fourth or last man was detected and if one of the boys had not caught the uplifted axe, there would have been one riderless horse. The woman captured the piece of bacon, however, and we rode off. I asked John if this kind of work had been going on long, and he said: "Yes, and that this woman was in fine fix, compared to some," if she and her hideout husband were all the family, and from seeing only one bed he guessed it was.

The cavalry moved about soon after this, but soon left the country, or at least a part of it. We received orders to get three days' rations and be ready to march and it was well impressed that we were to pass through a barren region, with few settlers, but the chances were we would be harrassed at favorable points by the jayhawkers and to be sure and provide well for horses as we would have a long and hard march before striking a supply, and there would be no foraging allowed and straggling to the rear would be sure death. It was said the conscript act had put nearly all the liable ones on the dodge, of a large section of East Tennessee and that there were but few killed or captured; therefore, there must be a great number hid in the mountains and the officers felt the seriousness of the march and the men felt how would they feel and what would they do if they were in the jayhawkers' shoes, standing trembling in the cold, dodging from place to place, with once a comfortable home, but fearing to go to it to pass the night; and if they did, to find about all the food necessities gone. This condition was not wholly confined to the Union man, as the country was looked upon as a Union country, and there seemed to be no lines drawn. As I reported for duty, some time after camp was struck, I cannot say that there was any general order to that effect, but eating the country out was practiced by a continuous divide and I guess often with little regard to a fair half. In gathering the three days' rations by the company's detail, there was yet a spark of human feeling left in both officers and privates of the battling front. I was in Company E's foraging squad, commanded by the sergeant, and we had gone quite a distance with no success, as the continuous dividing process had left only a pittance with a barren and frozen country as a fore and background, without animal to ride or slaughter. We were much disgusted and discouraged. To our front and right, about a fourth of a mile we discovered a squad larger than ours. We went to them and found a lieutenant in charge. Our officer inquired of the lieutenant the cause of waiting. His reply was: "There are thirty or forty bushels of corn" and some fodder in a barn loft which was standing near by, and from the great number of women and children who were at the house he could not make up his mind to take it without different orders and that he had sent couriers some time since with a report and was awaiting orders. The sergeant ordered us to dismount and wait for a reply, so there was a mixing and talking. Some of the boys who had been at the house said that there had been four sitting at the table for breakfast and gave the number of women and children, and if I recollect right, it was near thirty, and I heard the remark that there was a bushel of corn and a bundle of fodder apiece, and there was a low murmur heard of their now sad plight, as they claimed that that was all they had as a whole. The orders came to "Take it;" and there was a rush and scramble filling sacks and grabbing fodder. When I was satisfied, I climbed down to make room for others. This went on until all were satisfied or the supply exhausted and the query when my detail rode off, was: "Was there any left?" and it was the general opinion, "Little, if any." When we charged the pile, as it were, the women and children came running and screaming in agony, but their appeals were not heeded. When I got out of the scramble and noise of the men, returning with my booty to my horse, I could hear from the appeals of the mother to an allwise and merciful God that they were not of the cursing and abusive kind; and I thought of the saying that everything goes in war, but it should be qualified by excepting prayer, as I had been taught that God would answer prayer that came from the heart, and if there ever was prayer offered that emanated from the soul these poor women had none or it was not in hearing, as it were of a just God. But my views have since been that one loaded gun in hand would have been more effective than the prayers of all the mothers and the crying and begging of the children. I have often thought—where did the orders emanate from, if any, that held a corps of men, if such, without any apparent restraint in a country to be overrun and the food supply consumed to starve out, as it were, a few Union men who would have been a burden to the fighting ranks, and why does man in his dictatorial powers assume the role of God and bring down punishment upon the helpless innocent to correct the errors of others? Seeing conditions as I did caused me to think how unfortunate one was to have his earthly holdings in a section of country that was treated as a part of East Tennessee was, during the Civil War and other sections passed over by the invader, and it was all done to free the negro; and when done by the flow of blood, three out of four of the liberators cared not a copper for the freedom of the negro; and about the same proportion on the Southern side did not give a damn. It was all caused by unbalanced leaders and the ignorant masses following to a point that history will show that there was one generation of warriors reared in this country; and it was fortunate for other governments that we got enough of the bloodspilling business at home. I often think of how fortunate the generation before and after were, for it was a question that had to be settled at some time and it was simply a repetition of history that boasted educated christianized man still retains his savage ancestor's law that "might is right."

Leaving this section, we passed through well closed up, a rough and barren country, with but few settlers: and as far as

I knew, with no attempt by bushwhackers or jayhawkers,* as they were commonly called, to harrass our line of march, though at times in the mountain gaps one or more could have created great confusion with but little danger to self, if he kept his foothold as his greatest danger was plunging downward. We were not long on this move before there was all the active service to perform that one could desire. We were retarding the enemy's advance, at times at the front flank or rear, and I assure you, there was always a job ahead. There are but few instances, however, (for want of memory) that I will attempt to describe. My first brush with the enemy was on their rear, near Kingston, Georgia. We charged a wagon train guard composed of cavalry. I was very desirous of getting a good horse and side arms, and to do so I knew the head fellow had the best chance, so at the order, "Charge," I plunged forward, firing carbine with no heed to alignment. I was soon near fifty yards to the front and was in near as much danger of being shot from rear as front, but my anxiety was such that the position was not a consideration. Just as I heard the words: "Keep in line" shouted, my horse was struck in the breast and fell and I was thrown off and well mixed with the dust, as the place I struck was well supplied. I was up instantly, brushed my eyes with my hand, then looking to the front saw the enemy fleeing—to my front and about one hundred yards lay a Yank on his stomach, stretched at full length. I made a run for him, but a mount well armed who did not need the pistol, beat me to it. I procured the fellow's spurs, but had to sit on his legs to hold them still

---

* "Bushwhackers" refers to men who had been hiding out in the woods and could attack from the bush. "Jayhawkers" were men skilled in guerrilla warfare tactics.

while removing. By the time I had them off his kicking and groaning days were over. I returned to my horse and found it standing up, saw it was struck in the lower part of the neck, but was not bleeding badly and could walk with but little apparent pain. I led it to the rear—one of the boys let me have a captured horse to ride, and as we slowly retraced our steps I had but little difficulty in keeping up. Night came on, and I guess it was as dark as they ever get in any part of the world, as eyes at any distance were useless and the way we kept close up in march was by those in our immediate front, when they starting to move, saying: "Forward." My wounded horse fell, and in falling the lead line was jerked from my hand. I dismounted, holding the bridle reins and started a search for my horse. I soon found this was a failure, as I or the horse would be run into by the moving animals. I remembered seeing a light a short distance from the road not far to the rear, so I led well out of the road and started forward in an opposite direction by sound of the march, feeling and slowly groping my way. I soon saw the light and made for it, got a torch, mounted and soon found my wounded horse, and was moving in column. We had captured quite a lot of prisoners, and wagons and teams; and I thought there would be few prisoners, if any, in sight next morning; but from appearances they were all there and I thought they must be of other stock than ours or they would have known the darker the night the better. My horse did not have a serious wound; was only weakened by loss of blood, so I was soon astride the old bay mare, equipped with a nice pair of spurs—was soon in the rear again, moving about lively. Tom Reaverly, one of Hood's Brigade transfers, and I were on the lookout for a mount and had a permit. I made three swaps on the trip and Tom made seven. My first swap was just across the road from a residence that the column was moving in and it was night—I had gone into the barn lot and changed horse. Just as I was riding in column, the old man had discovered me and had gotten through the column, grabbed my reins and said "Woo-woo, I thought it took two to make a trade." Just as I said: "You ain't read up, old man," one of the boys jammed his horse on him and he turned loose. The last I heard of him one would think if he had been knocked down, would he have taken the hint? The next time I swapped it was near the edge of a small town, I taking a nice, sleek mule. It was night and the woman of the place heard us and was soon on the scene, dressed in white, and she sure said enough—at times her words were such that I guess she forgot she was a preacher's wife, or at least that was used in her pleadings. The horse I left was a good one, but too slow for cavalry service. We rode through the town and found a scouting party camped. It was in charge of one of Company "E's" lieutenants. We stopped for the night. The next morning, bright and early, a woman was at camp and reported me to the officer. He claimed no authority in the matter and told her it was my duty to keep well mounted if the stock was in the country to press. She appealed to me and I agreed to return, if she would tell me the hiding of some good horse near by. She made me promise not to mention information, then she gave me the hiding place of three good horses about two miles out in a small opening in a bushy surrounding. As I passed back through town I could hear on every side of the street: "There goes the fellow who stole the mule." We found the place where the horses had been, from signs—but none were to be found. We dismounted at a fence that enclosed the small opening, and as a shed was near far side, walked in. I was some distance ahead of Pard, and not expecting an attack from any direction; so when nearing the shelter there was a boy stepped from hiding in the path, between Pard and me. He had a small rifle, and I don't suppose he had seen Pard—the first I knew was when Pard said: "Drop that gun." When I looked around he had dropped it. We left the old gun, but took the boy and started toward the residence, which was about half a mile away. We struck a plum orchard near the house and were sitting on our horses, eating greedily of the fruit when we were 'spied by the man of the house. He was near us before he made himself known, raising a racket about our impudence and such like. We discovered a pistol, on the Colt's order, in his pocket and made him deliver. We ordered him to stand with our other prisoner and when we finished satisfying our wants, told the boy to return to his gun, but not to start our way again with it in his hand. We told the old man to move to the front and to obey orders. We instructed him to go to the back yard gate near by and to open same. He did so, and we told him to proceed to the front gate. In doing this we passed near the house just at the opportune time. He darted forward; Tom spurred his horse to the door, entered, and I was quickly at an open window, and almost as quick as a flash he had placed a chair by the wall, then in it, with his hand on a gun that was in a rack that was too high for him to reach from the floor. Two voices rang out: "Hands off!" The old fellow twisted his neck so he could see, and lowered his hand and came out as ordered. He opened the gate; we rode off with him in company as prisoner. He, by this time, had cooled down and was talking with better judgment. He wanted the return of his fine repeating pistol, and would do most anything to get it. I proposed that if he would tell me where there was a good horse, and I succeeded in getting it, and it was not too far off, I would return and give him his pistol. He readily consented and gave directions which were about one and a half miles off. We turned him loose, and had no trouble in finding the place, and sure enough there was coming our way in a plow, the horse described. We were at the front gate. I made our business known—man hooted at the idea of trade. I told him it would be of short duration, as we were on the enemy's flank and rear and were raiding their rear; and as we would return out that way, he could get his horse back in a week or so, possibly well tired; as my horse was as good as his, if rested up, there could be but little difference. He read the hand-writing on the wall and slowly but grumbling, unharnessed. I was soon in the saddle with no intent of looking for others to devour, as Tom and I were well mounted. While making the trade, the mother with a bevy of nice girls came up and put in their protests, but I could not rue, as I had closed the trade at first sight. This was what one would call pressing by owner's consent. This animal proved all that one could desire. We were soon at the front again and found the enemy slowly but surely moving forward as some great serpent with its prey ahead, at times sending forth its fiery red tongue. Our army was contesting every inch of ground, both night and day. The enemy with good cavalry force, raided our rear. I was on detail at the time, and John Pipkin and I were some distance out on outpost duty. We received instructions through a hurried courier that the enemy was raiding our rear and to locate them as soon as possible and that the detail would follow. We pushed hurriedly in the direction indicated and after traveling several miles we came to a burned bridge, but could not determine by which army it had been burned. We soon found a crossing and were beyond the bridge in the road about half a mile, when we discovered, a few hundred yards to our right, a mass of moving beings. We started in their direction, with houses in front that would screen our approach, with no thought of rear, in case of a hurried retreat. We made the desired point about two hundred and fifty yards from the moving body and found it to be a mixture of mounted enemy and negroes, with every conceivable mode of transportation. John and I concluded to have a little fun by shooting at the mounted enemy, not caring a straw whether we hit a negro or not. We turned loose with our carbines, three charges each—terror reigned, and there was as if by magic, a dismounting, jumping from carts and wagons; and I guess there were a number of mothers who forgot their babes, and grandmas and grandpas who forgot, for the time, that there was such a thing as rheumatism. John and I were enjoying the fun immensely, looking only for an attack from the front. The road that we had come in on intersected road the enemy was on, and our attention was soon attracted by the charging enemy's noise to our left and rear, on this road. We turned to our right at speed, with bullets coming our way. We soon struck a wooded, boggy flat, about one hundred yards wide. We had no choice of direction, but plunged through under the force of spurs and a rain of bullets, with our horses belly deep in the mud. This had retarded our speed and from the number of the enemy at close distance, it was remarkable that we made our escape without a scratch. Just after crossing the bog we were on a steep up-grade for a short distance and at the brow of the hill was a worm rail fence. The bullets were yet raining. John dismounted to tear down the fence. I called to him to mount, just as I threw the weight of my horse against it. The fence flattened and John and I were soon out of bullet's reach, with no enemy attempting to follow. The mud was now to our advantage; and I guess there was not a horse in their bunch that would have made it through unless it was in the lead, as ours. We were soon at the top of a good elevation and in sight of our boys on the opposite side of the stream that the burned bridge crossed. Hearing the noise that John and I had started, made all the report necessary. My horse, when I stopped, gave signs of complete let down, and apparently was badly thumped. John's horse, which was of mouse color and a Texas Mustang and which he had when I joined him in East Tennessee, was consuming everything eatable near, apparently no worse for the wear. I had often scolded him for the unnecessary hard rides and little care he would give his horse; and when I would get after him he would say: "Bill, it makes no difference, you can't kill him." Seeing my well groomed and kept horse trembling and breathing fast, I said: "John, look at that D—— horse." His reply was: "I guess you will let me alone hereafter, and believe me." In the course of thirty minutes we concluded my horse was worse scared than hurt; mounted and rode off in the direction of the enemy's travel; heard at times some shooting, knew that our scouts were retarding their movement and keeping them bunched as much as possible. On the second day we met one of our boys who was one of the scattered crowd, as we were trying to retard until our forces could come up to force battle. He knew nothing of our fighting force, but said: "Boys," and pointing to a house that was in sight, some distance away, "they were crowding a bunch of Yankees and they ran into the house to fortify, but Clem Basset* was so near that by the time they got in and closed the doors, he had his six-shooter at a crack and downed four, before they surrendered." Clem had the reputation of always having a full hand when called.

Our forces soon met the enemy and they took to the woods, and their position was a very favorable one for them. They were held by being harrassed in the timber, making no effort to escape, but strictly on the defense. Our forces, I suppose, were near equal, or our officers expected a surrender, or we would have forced the fight. Night came on, and some-time during the night the enemy passed out; and, from re-ports, there were found in the water holes of a small stream in the woods quite a number of pistols. They crossed the river a few miles off from the point of the day's hiding and it was swimming. From reports, they disposed of a lot of pistols in crossing the river. Some of the boys were said to have made a good haul by diving. We were soon in front again, and kept well occupied. Here was where I had my first experience of dismounting to fight. We were dismounted and thrown some distance ahead. The enemy seemed to be in good force, and from the roar and hail of bullets, we concluded we had struck a line armed with sixteen-shooters. We did not venture near or remain long, before we were ordered to fall back and mount. This order is always promptly and quickly obeyed, as the average cavalryman feels near half-whipped if he has to leave his horse any great distance, to fight. We were not held

---

* *History of Fort Bend County*, by A. J. Sowell, published in Houston in 1904, gives a short biography of Clement Newton "Clem" Bassett on page 366. He was born at Richmond, Texas, on January 7, 1842. In September 1861, he was sworn into Terry's Texas Rangers at Houston.

at the front duties long, and soon turned up in the enemy's rear in considerable force, destroying the railroad where it could be done with little or no resistance. Our worst resistance was what were called "block houses," and we generally found them at the streams or openings where bridging or trestling, if destroyed, would cause much delay in traffic. Block houses were built of small logs notched down, with holes in the wall to shoot through, and were stationed at a point to best protect the structure, if attempted destruction. The country was fairly well supplied with worm rail fencing near one or both sides of the railroad track. We were moved in column of regiments near the side of the road and when the desired point had been reached, we were halted, generally fronting toward the road, dismounted—every fourth man holding the horses, and the balance put to carrying fence rails and placing them on each side of the rail on one side of the track. Six or eight rails all well connected would make sufficient heat when fired, to bend the rails by expansion, and ruin the ties. When a regiment had completed its front, it would move to front of column and repeat the same performance, and as there was a large body of us, by this method we destroyed during twenty-four hours a good mileage of track; but at all times, as far as I knew, we kept clear of the block house sharp shooters. At points where there were no fence rails and cordwood was handy, we would use it. At night, on long straight pieces of track the sight of the long line of fire looked beautiful to the destroyer. This was a long and laborious raid, and both man and horse were well worn when it terminated. My plow animal proved rather an exception and was among the least worn at the outcome, and my horse and the one rode by Fox Trammel did more than their portion the last few days of company detail, yet Trammel's horse was said to have been drawn by him at first service and was not in the hands of a good master. It was said that we treated about five hundred miles of road in Sherman's rear in this way. We were, at one time, what was called five days and nights in the saddle—which was not unsaddling. When we could, we fed our horses twice a day—at such times we could cook, eat or get sleep; but our labor was nearly continuous, without unsaddling, for that length of time. One would do fairly well for sleep if he could nap while riding, which the most of us did. I had a funny experience the first night after the five days. The order was passed along the marching column that we would go into camp for the night, and not knowing at what point our regiment would turn out or the amount of the delay before it did, I proposed to one of the company's boys that we increase our pace and ride up one side of the moving column and the first place we struck where the men were camping to turn in. We did this, and dismounted in a small enclosure—found the same wet and muddy. There were several small logs on the ground and they were in one layer, touching each other, which made a log flooring four or five feet wide. They had been in this position some time, as was evidenced by vegetable growth that had come up between them. This we mashed down; we spread on two blankets, stretched a small fly tent about 5 × 7 feet, to protect from rain. The horses cared for, we were soon between the blankets and the night was drizzling rain, and twilight. When we crawled in we heard a buzzing noise under our blankets and thought we were over a bumblebees' nest but were soon asleep—for how long, I don't know. I was awakened by the bees stinging me. I rolled out in a hurry, gave Pard a punch and told him to get up, as the bees were out in force and would sting him. He grunted, and mumbled out something which, I guess if it had been clearly and distinctly said, I would not have understood for the bees were under my clothing and in the hair of my head, as well as on the outside; and I was busy ridding my person and clothing of them and yet, with all the haste I could summon, I got well stung. After getting rid of them I was agreeably surprised at the short duration of pain that followed the sting. The cause must have been the condition of a well-tired and worn body. The bees were of the large white-back kind and were generally classed as the next stinger, in point of pain, to the hornet. I wanted to move; but Pard, from his soundness of sleep, was all right; and as I had asked him to follow me and I would divide shelter for the night, I could not remove it; and as it was rather damp to be without it, I concluded to try it again, so I pulled out the covering blanket and rid it of the bees, wrapped it around me and crawled under the roofing. I tucked the blanket around my feet, and covered head and hands well, and thought I was safe from further attack. I considered that I had not wronged Pard and from his motionless body, under the existing conditions, one would suppose he was near lifeless—so much so, that I thought he had the bees fooled, for they will not sting unless there are signs of life; and the more and faster one moves seems to suit them better. I do not know how long I lay undisturbed in my supposed safe protection. I must have laid very quiet, for when I awoke there was quite a number of bees stinging me, on nearly all parts of my body at the same time. I suppose they thought of me as they did of Pard, or there could not have been the number that was under my clothing without waking me earlier. I have often thought my death-like sleep fooled them, and when on their rambles some one or more struck a point of pulsation and found their mistake, and stung me, and under the pain I moved, and all that were in position were put on notice. I sure was well stung before I could rid my body of the pest; but fortunately, as at the first attack, the pain was soon gone and I found no swelling. The bees did not attempt to fly, but were good walkers and, from their white backs, could be seen a short distance in the twilight. Pard was yet on his back, and I guess had not moved a limb from his first position when he entered the shelter. I could only hear him breathe when near and listening. I went to his side of the tent to experiment, as I thought it was clear of bees. This I knew was not the case on my side, for I had carried them out. I could neither see nor hear any on his side from under the roof, but they were crawling at will over his body. I knelt near his side and with my finger thumped and pressed on exposed part of his body until I got stung, then I got a short piece of weed and opened his shirt bosom; so after trying all parts of the exposed or naked body, and not seeing one twitch or hearing as much as a sigh, I thought the test was completed—that bees would not sting him or had taken him for dead—and I thought the saying "dead asleep" would have been well applied to this subject. I concluded to leave Pard in his glory and try other quarters, so I spent the balance of the night on top of a near by rail fence—by placing two rails side by side and rolling up in my blanket and lying on my stomach and using my arms for pillows. The ground was too wet and sloppy to lay on, when there was better accommodation so easily arranged. One without experience may think that such lodging is imaginary—if so, get your physical and mental condition right and make a test and you will for a time, enjoy it. I was soon asleep, with no fear of oversleeping. I awoke and was up at dawn—had fly tent down; had given Pard a few punches (he was not so hard to arouse) told him to get up for mercy sake and move his horse a good distance off, as the bees would soon be on the wing and would sting him. As for myself and horse, we would soon be well out of danger; and we were. He said he knew nothing after he fell asleep until just then; and if stung, was not aware of it. We were now making for a crossing on Tennessee River and when reached, we forded it at night. It was wide and swift at the place of crossing, and my horse got his feet or legs foul and was washed down by the current—horse and rider both went under, but I stuck to the saddle, and the horse was soon up again. When we had crossed the river there was a sigh of relief and a feeling of pride in our accomplishments. We thought Sherman's army would be put to their wits end and possibly fall back to their base of supplies, but such was not the case, for when we swung around near his front it did not take one with much intellect to see that one of the greatest rear raids of the war was a failure, for we could hear the rumble of the trains, as usual; and it was said we did nothing to cause hunger to either man or beast, or create a shortage in the supply of ammunition. It was said that Sherman was expecting the raid and was well supplied with all the necessities and had all the men and material at hand to repair the damage to transportation nearly as fast as done, so instead of using his army to battle in the rear, he was slowly but surely advancing—while we were exhausting our efforts in the rear. We struck the enemy after recrossing the river, on their right and rear, and were one day feeling our way to their front. Upon finding their whereabouts we commenced slowly falling back. The enemy were following, but there was little firing by either side, and that, at long range. I, with some others, had passed in a scattered condition over a piece of woodland well set with undergrowth. I stopped in the

woods, about fifty yards from an opening I could see to the
front, as there was no order of alignment, and the distance
between us was at times so great that one could not see the
right or left man in the thick underbrush, and hearing was
somewhat of a guide to alignment. I heard, to my right rear,
a noise; took it to be one of our men. The idea struck me
that I was too far to the front and I was waiting for the man
to get to my right, and then move on. From the sound, I
knew the man would come into alignment with me at about
one hundred feet distance. I had turned my horse so I was
looking nearly straight to that point and was in this position
a short time when the riders rode up and were looking
straight forward, and had observed the opening to their front.
I instantly saw that I was too far to the rear or the riders were
too far to the front. At the point of the halt, the opening in
the brush between us was sufficient to clearly see. I instantly
had cocked, and raised gun—for their uniform, at a glance,
was sufficient. The two riders stopped, side by side, and the
one nearest me was a boy about the size, or less, than the one
whom I have mentioned among the dead at Fredericksburg.
I saw I could not hit the man without shooting through the
boy and I thought if, by chance, I could shoot the man down
without injury to the boy, that he would force me to kill him
in self defense. When these ideas had flashed through my
mind the thought of possible remorse caused me to lower my
gun, turn horse, and spur him at quick time to their left and
enter the opening some distance to their left front. When I
entered the opening, I saw our men well to the front. I have
often thought of this occurrence. I cannot say, with pride,
however; for I was holding individual remorse above duty to
my country.

Capture and Escape

THE NEXT INCIDENT of note was in battle line, near Rome, Georgia; and from what I could see, the rangers were detached from the other cavalry. We were lined up in an open field with a thick underbrush and timber growth not far to our rear, and in front a short distance there seemed to be a stream or water drain from the timber appearance. And beyond, for a considerable distance, there was an open field, and on the far side of this field and near the timber, we could plainly see the enemy's infantry forming in battle line; and we thought they were preparing to advance, so I guess all eyes were to the front, with no thought of flank, for the first warning we had of being flanked by the enemy's cavalry was their nearness and the charging and shooting at our right, and as we were formed at right angle to the main road that we had come in on, we were, to a great extent, cut off from the road and the greater part of the Rebs in their flight took to the woods, or to the near country or farm road and were soon strung out in the road, making the best run they could in single or double file, and the Yanks were in close pursuit, running about in the same order as we were. I heard some firing on the main road and from that and the direction we were running our road ran nearly parallel to the public road. I heard no attempt to form and fight, and I afterwards learned that the run was made to prevent the enemy from cutting us off from the mountain gap. The distance from start to finish, was said to be about nine miles, but the Rebs got to the gap first and stopped—the longest run, I guess, the Terry boys were ever in. Soon after we entered the farm road, I dropped to the rear and commenced what is called firing on retreat. As the brush at places was so thick, there were but few men in action at times; and often not more than two. The enemy seemed to be cheered by catching us napping and were making every effort to crowd us, but had to keep to the road, so their advance guard had none the advantage of our rear guard. After emptying my carbine, I spurred up the line and reloaded, and was checking at favorable places to be at or near the rear so I could come into action when I thought I could render service. This was my first opportunity while in cavalry to get into a scrap of the kind and as I knew there was no special rear guard for the occasion, therefore, it was a free for all business, and as all the other fellows had opportunities before, it made me rather greedy to be in the rear when I could have as well kept my place in line. At a point where there were but few men to the rear of me, and my horse was going at a sweeping lope, it put both forefeet into a hole that was made by the rotting of a stump, but did not fall; but while in the act of recovering, it was struck by a near horse and thrown on its side, my left foot and leg were under the horse, but both feet clear of stirrup. I grabbed the bridle reins near the bit with my left hand and at each effort of the horse to get up it was struck, but I hung to the rein and was fortunate enough not to be trampled upon. In my animal's last effort to rise, it was across the road on its knees, and I was on one hand and knees; and in this position I was knocked loose from my hold on the reins by a rear horse, which was a large dark bay or brown, rode by a lieutenant. The horse, in passing the head of my horse, struck me about the center of the forehead with its right fore leg. I fell back, and saw stars, as it were. I was stretched full length on my back with my head from the enemy and my hand loose from the rein. As I arose I saw two Yanks in sight, coming my way. I turned, running; saw my horse fleeing at good speed. I was a moderately fast runner, especially when scared. I thought I could overtake our rear, but they fast left me—and from the noise behind, I knew the Yanks were gaining. They were not shooting, but were having their fun at my expense, yelling: "Run you Rebel S—— of a B——. Hide out; we will catch you, Johnnie," and such like. From the noise, I knew they were gaining fast; but I did not have time to look around. My mind at this time was concentrated on one point only, and that was, run—had no thought of surrender, or overtaking our men, as hope in that direction had gone; it was run, run. The noise behind indicated their nearness and urging of horses that they were going to run over me. They had never said surrender, and I had no mind that there was such a thing. My first thought of realization was the attempt to run over me and their horses' heads were near my back when this thought struck me. I sprang to my right instantly—the right horse cleared me about a foot—the rider could have knocked me down, if he had been expecting the move. The right man fired first and as their horses were near speed, the smoke passed to the front and right. The left man fired over the rump of the right horse, but from the smoke of the first shot,

I did not note the direction the ball passed. The next thought was to fall; the next to lie still; the next—I am not hit or I would have heard shot. I was laying on my right side with my feet nearest the road looking the way I was running. I had come to my senses now enough to hurriedly think and plan; had eyes near closed—saw the two Yanks rein up; heard noise behind; the two Yanks turned and started to me. Just then an officer with a squad of twenty or thirty came up. The officer halted the squad, gave the two men a good cursing for stopping to prowl dead Rebs when the fighting line were near by, and threatened them with punishment, or any others he caught; ordered them on at speed and he gave the command: "Forward," and dashed ahead—the officer was but a minute halting, cursing and moving. I could hear a noise to the rear and knew that others were coming, and took chances as the squad passed, of any of them looking back. Just at my back, with limbs to the road, stood a scrubby oak tree, several inches in diameter. At the ground the foliage was thick and some of it was near or resting on the ground. I quickly crawled under and lay drawn up on the opposite side of the body of the tree, face to the road. The second squad soon passed at a good speed—there were nearly two hundred in this body. The firing now was quite a distance off—heard a roaring to the rear and was satisfied that it was the enemy's main force. I looked for other hiding; saw about two hundred feet from the road a good sized uprooted tree; was soon on the opposite side, laying flat, with my body well wedged under the curve of the log. By quick work, I just had time to avoid detection. I lay in this position while a large troop of cavalry passed at full loping speed. When their rear had passed, I raised up and looked well to the rear for stragglers —saw none, neither did I much expect it, for the distance the main body was behind the advance caused me to think they were fearful of an ambuscade. After they had all passed, I went to opposite the place where I was dismounted. I kept well to the side of the road, in brush, cautiously going to the point and seeing no straggling enemy, was soon on and over full fifty yards of the road that horse and I had been thumped over, picking up such articles as were to be seen of the wreck; found a piece of tobacco and a silver spoon, that I got near the pontoon bridge on the Rappahannock, also my carbine, and it looked to be unharmed, and I took it to be in perfect order, and I knew it was freshly loaded, so I pronounced it good and that I was in luck. All other earthly effects, less clothes on my body, were gone; so, as it were, I must make a new start in life. I was soon in the foot hills, making fair time in the direction of my command; saw, during daylight, several small squads of the enemy roaming the country. When night came, I left the foot hills and took my chances on more level ground, but followed down the mountain range. I did not see or hear the enemy during night tramp; struck our outpost on the road, passed near them unobserved, and found my command at the entrance of the mountain gap. The next morning I got leave of absence to remount. Before leaving camp, some of the boys gave me two light home-spun spreads, as they were called, and a Yankee rubber rain proof which was of size about four by five feet, with a hole in the center for one's head. So, with a freshly loaded carbine and a few extra cartridges, and well housed from the cold or rain, I was soon near the enemy's picket line across the river from Rome. I was several days scouting near, before I made an attempt to mount. The Yanks during the time sent out several foraging parties, but they were too large and kept so near bunched up that I saw no favorable chance of getting a horse. While on this bum I met two fellows who had seen no service, but who were anxious to. From their talk I guessed them to be sincere—they both had good guns; so I told them I would give them a trial and help mount them, provided they would faithfully obey orders. They promised, and as they were well versed in the surroundings, I was soon advised of the best mode of procedure and the best way to retreat when going out mounted. I took my time and in fact was taking advantage of my liberty, and as the Yanks had not treated that section brutally, there was plenty to eat at all the places at which I stopped; but all the stock was taken that was fit for work or food; but no other depredations or abuses heard of, less the use of fencing for fires. I was at and near the place several times where I was dismounted. Near by lived a widow—her family consisted of two daughters and one son. She had been a resident of Rome, but had moved out when the enemy took possession. I stayed one night at this house, and was told of the Rebel stampede and the enemy's close pursuit; and on their return there was a search made for a dead Reb who had been killed nearby on the side of the road, and they accused them of hiding the body, as they knew they had killed him for one of them had placed his gun against his head and fired, and the other had plugged him in the breast as he fell, and they knew he was dead for they stopped and looked at him and said they were going to prowl him and have evidence to show what they had done, but the officer came up too quick and made them go on. The family were curious if it was as they said, as none of the near neighbors knew of a newly made grave. When they got through, I asked if they knew of a hole in the road just in sight of the house and they said "Yes, where a stump had rotted." I asked how far it was from that point to the dead Reb and they said about three hundred yards further up from what the Yankees said. They were somewhat surprised when I told them to make no further inquiry about the newly made grave, for I was the corpse. While on this outing, I was often separated from the boys and they followed instructions, as far as I knew; and that was not to fire a gun, only in self defense; to take no prisoners as we could not get them out; to keep well concealed from the enemy or anyone that they knew would inform on us, for our only object was to mount, but not to undertake it where we were not sure of success. I could have, upon more than one occasion, turned out butchering stock from enclosure at night, but thought it would possibly have done harm instead of good, as the Yanks would have recovered the most of them and held it against the near by settlers. I could have made captives of some of their infantry, but kept out of sight. In about a week's time I got my forces together and explained my plans, which were, to capture the two out-riding pickets. This, I found to be the custom on one of the main roads, that when the two men on post were relieved they rode to the front on the road about one-fourth of a mile and at once returned. So we came down through brush, between river and road to a favorable point, as the two Yanks passed going out, we secreted ourselves near the side of the road. This was done late in the evening, so the enemy's chances of pursuit were not good. The boys were to take the off rider and pay no attention to the near, as I would take him. I had cautioned them to be sure and not shoot, as we were nearly in sight of their pickets and their detail was but a short distance in the rear. One of the boys was to go to the rear and the other to the front, just as I ordered them to halt and hold up their hands; and mount horse, when rider was disarmed and dismounted. At the proper time, as the Yanks were returning with no apparent thought of the enemy, I stepped out to the front and they obeyed orders. The boys went to the proper place and the front one had the horse by the bridle rein near bits, but were greatly excited and the Yank, seeing this, was courageous enough to stick spurs to his horse and turn and run off, and they both shot off their guns when the Yank was at least fifty yards off, and I was saying: "Don't shoot." I don't think I ever saw a person lose his senses and go to pieces as badly as those two kids did. My prisoner was disarmed and dismounted in short order and was in front, running to the rear with the boys. I halted them when at a safe distance out, and went through the Yank's pockets; got a good silver watch and some tobacco and swapped boots with him; then turned him loose and told him he could report for duty. I mounted one of the boys on the horse and instructed him to take it home which was several miles off and hide out—and to have him attended to, and to return and look us up. The Yank was about as excited as the boys, but seemed to be much relieved when told to go. The Yank had no side arms, which I regretted, as I had, up to this time, failed to procure any, but had no need for them, as the carbine so far had been all I had needed. I saw but few negroes during the war, with U.S.A. uniform on; but on this tramp just out from the picket line late one evening I arrested one—he thought he would surely meet death, and commenced begging. I told him to quiet down and tell the truth, and I would let him go. I asked him several questions in regard to the enemy's position in and about Rome and some of them I knew to be correct; I thought all his answers were about as he understood conditions. He claimed to be a servant and had gotten permission to go out and see some colored people near by and did not think of seeing a Reb. He promised to say nothing about our meeting and gave me his knife and tobacco for the mere asking. I advised him in future to keep well in his line of blue and turned him loose. He was very profuse in his thanks. The next morning after the capture of the horse, one of the boys and I were some miles up the river, looking for a favorable place to swim horses, as I knew of the cavalry camps on the opposite side, and that the enemy only watched the most favorable places. I was hunting a good outcome on the bank from them, where they were not guarding; had found the same, but was looking further to see if we could find a better place. We were so far above town that we had no thought of meeting the enemy and were walking in a country wagon road that nearly paralleled the river. My plan was to swim the river at night, although the water was cold. I knew I could keep part of my clothing dry and was going to leave the balance, also my gun with Pard, on the home side, at the selected crossing; and I was going to try my luck in making a sneak steal of two horses and equipment and putting them across the stream. I was confident that I could do it at the proper time at night when the camp fires were low and all was quiet, but while walking in the road mentioned, all was lost; for there appeared to our front, about four hundred yards up the road three well mounted Yanks. As soon as they saw us they put spurs to their horses and commenced firing. I jumped behind a tree and fired and told Pard to protect and fight. He sure did protect but did not fire a shot. His tree of protection was fully two hundred yards out from the road, although he passed numbers equally as good. After my first shot I could not reload. I tried in vain and was so intent that the Yanks were on three sides and near, with guns pointing and holloaing to drop the gun or they would kill me. They fired several shots while coming my way, but all went wild of the mark—if I was the intended one. They saw my earnest but helpless condition and seemed to have no thought of bodily injury, if they could avoid it. After I dropped the gun, they called Pard in and had considerable sport out of his cowardly run. One of the Yanks said to me: "Look here, Reb, you must be a good shot. See this hair cut and ear burn? You did it; and you are lucky it is no worse, or we would have killed you. The ear don't bleed, but the upper part burns like the mischief." We were ordered to leave our guns and mount behind. We did so and they were off in a lope. I was now reflecting on my condition and the cause of my gun not working, as I had carried it for some time and it had never failed to work promptly. The idea struck me that it was put out of order when the horse fell, in the stampede, and was run over by the cavalry. I then thought that when I picked up the gun I pronounced it uninjured, knew it was loaded and had magazine full, but gave it no minute inspection and that it had not been fired up to that time, so I felt I had no one to blame but myself for carelessness, as I thought I could have unmanned each horse if gun would have worked, but such was then to be my fate, the always dreaded confinement of a prisoner. Our captors were young, courageous, but inexperienced soldiers, made no unkind or taunting remarks, they seemed to have no thought of attempted escape or they surely would have rode different from what they did. The two that had prisoners behind them should have paired and rode ahead, but several times I and my mount were behind and near up to the front couple and each had an army Colt's in his belt and I saw how easy I could get possession of the one that was so near me and with it I could give my man a dead shot or a stunning blow, and at least shoot one of the front men before they could fire with any degree of correctness, and would have an even go with the third. All this would revolve through my mind and I also thought of the brutality of such an act perpetrated on men who had shown themselves not to be of the abusive or bloodthirsty kind; and there was Pard with his back to me, to consider; for, in the effort, if started, I might kill him, although I felt I would have been better off if some one had done it long since—for I thought the beastly coward needed killing, but I could not take the chances of doing it. I would feel at times that I would be better dead than in prison, and would, at times, feel that I was near the point of desperation. Then a little reasoning would say: all wrong; it would be brutal. So I went for some distance with this feeling and I cannot to this day say whether it was fear of committing an uncalled for brutal act, or was it pure cowardice that I did not attempt to escape. I had two similar instances to happen soon after. One I did not attempt, for the other fellow weakened, but the mind conditions were similar. The third one was all to self and was accomplished and mind strain was similar. Our captors were true to what was said to be General Sherman's teaching, that "War is hell," and the principle practiced was about the same, "Not to kill, but punish." When we had gone some distance, we were passing near settlers' places. They would shoot such animals as were near the roadside, and if they were dead shots, they did not prove it, as I only saw one fall; but they seemed to enjoy even to have hit the brute. I well remember one nice flock of sheep that were near the road and near the front of a residence. They each took several shots at the bunch of poor harmless brutes, and to see them squirm in agony, from laughter and remarks, one would at least suppose they were enjoying it. I had remonstrated several times before they struck the sheep, they taking it good naturedly; but did not heed. When they turned loose on the sheep, I said: "Boys, if you had done that in Texas, the owner would follow you to your grave, as they do a sheep killing dog; and I think one of the worst men we have in our company will not kill a sheep, when he is hungry; and if you live and are so fortunate as to ever live in Texas, don't tell this, or it will put you in bad repute." They took no offense, but laughed at my remarks. My pard's mother and aunt lived in Rome, and he was much mortified at being a prisoner, and was scared at his probable fate; as the Yanks soon found he was a weak subject and had no control over his fears, and was very anxious to explain. They put a number of questions to him, and got about a correct report of our doings. When we struck the main road, we were ordered to dismount and walk ahead— the road was wet and muddy. Pard and I were walking side by side and when the Yanks would ask a question and he would start to answer and explain, I would punch him with my elbow. They did not order me to desist, but seemed to enjoy the punching; so this left it with me to punch and curse at will, and several times I sent him staggering and groaning nearly across the road by a good hard elbow punch in the rib. I suppose the punishment was great for both of my elbows felt the effects of the blows, and I guess he got a fair share of pain; but with all this, he told that we were two of the party of three that had captured the picket and how it was done, and that I had given him the watch and he had left it with a friend, fearing that he would lose it, and stated the place the watch was; and started to tell at what point the horse could be found. I said to him in low tone: "If you tell, I will cut your throat." This upset him so that he made a denial of any knowledge of horse hiding as Charley had rode off with no special orders. I have often thought of those three young Yanks, and if it was not one of the incidents in their lives that they have told numbers of times. We crossed the river near the edge of town on a pontoon bridge and were taken near the center and put in the second story of a small house that had a step entrance outside, running with the side-walk and a good sized platform for a landing in front of the door. On this platform there was a guard and on the sidewalk below there was one who walked post length of the building. During the day the entrance door was left open at times, one or two prisoners would be permitted to stand on the platform and view the surroundings. I found in the prison fifteen or twenty prisoners, but if I remember correctly, there was not one of the old battling line boys. They were partly of the untrained, and partly belonging to no branch of the service; and were confined for some reported or supposed offense and were treated the same as prisoners of war. I soon got ac-quainted with a middle aged gentleman who was there for the great and heinous crime of aiding and sympathizing—if I remember correctly, he was not a native, but had been in that vicinity a number of years and was well versed in the surroundings and the loyalty of the people and he said they might as well imprison every white man, woman and child so far as his acquaintance went—if he had committed a pun-ishable offense. He and I soon got somewhat chummy—he had been there several days and well understood prison man-agement. I think I remained in this place five days and there was plenty of food provided; but I had no appetite and would eat but little. I was restless and was nearly all the time, when awake, building air castles of escape. I was standing on the platform about noon of the second day when I saw the pro-vost captain, whom I had learned by sight, coming my way with the man I recognized as the one I had captured and was then wearing his boots. I was fearful there was an investigation on, so I went back into the room and rolled bedding around me and laid down by the side of the wall, with all parts hid, and played asleep. I heard them ascending the steps and entering and a voice saying, "Look around and see if you can find him." I laid motionless, less the thumping of my heart, and I thought it was unusually noisy. I did not have to lay in this suspense long, when the covering was pulled from my head and a big Dutch form bending over me, saying in a brogue well drawn out: "Here he is, Cappitan." The captain ordered me up and asked me if I did not have on that man's boots. I said, "Yes, if he claims they are his, and they were mine when I claimed them under war custom." The captain's face showed a bland smile and he said: "Off with them boots." So in short order the exchange was made and I was on my feet. The captain then stated that he was going to turn me over to the cavalry regiment that my once prisoner belonged to, to be shot; as I had been reported of intent and acts of sufficient proof that I was going to put a prisoner to death and by mismanagement on my part he escaped. I stood motionless, with intent gazing on the face of my judge and jury while he pronounced sentence which, in my mind, was to be executed, as ordered. When he was through, he asked the green Dutch Yank if he had not correctly stated. Before he had time to reply, I had turned facing him, with uplifted fist, in a wild and maniacal rage, daring and cursing and calling him all hard names that my memory was gifted with. I said: "Speak, speak, and a damned liar's teeth go down his throat." The poor helpless being trembled and did not open his mouth. I think he was the most subdued subject I ever saw. The captain saw the pitiful condition of his man and spoke, and attracted my attention. I faced him in silence. He said he knew the man had reported correctly and he was going to turn me over to the regiment to be shot. The words were not more than out of his mouth when I said, in as calm a tone as I could command, "Captain, I am an honorable old line soldier, served in Hood's Texas Brigade in Virginia; was wounded twice; disabled from infantry duty; was transferred to Terry's Texas Rangers, and when you have shot me, you will have committed a crime that the Hood and Terry boys will liberally revenge, for under no conditions can you take me from this prison without publicity. If you desire secrecy, you had better shoot the whole bunch." He listened very courteously until I was through, and turned to walk out, remarking: "Your doom is sealed; I will have you shot." I bounded to his front, in wild rage; tore the front of my shirt bosom open saying: "Shoot, shoot, you damned Yankee, shoot," and pounded on my breast, with both fists, at quick motion, with rebound of fist nearly touching his nose, and all of the vile names and curse words that I knew, and there were many—he got them at lightning-like order. When I paused in my insane tirade he said: "If you don't hush, I will have you bucked and gagged." I turned, replying: "I will hush, for I know you are cowardly enough to have it done." He made no reply, and he and "Dutchy" were soon out of the room. I had thoroughly examined the prison before for a place of escape. I made another critical examination, but could see none so I went out on the stair landing and looked the surroundings well over—could see the river below, which was a few hundred yards off; could see no guard post from prison to the river, so I soon laid my plans of escape or death, as it might be, and not be shot down like a bound brute. I had worked myself up to make the attempt if I was not taken out of the prison before night. My plans were, to pallet near the opening of the door and to lay and watch my time for a break. The door was not locked generally at night, as the platform and the street sentinel were considered sufficient, so at the still of night I intended to carefully open the door enough to look through crack and at the opportune time, spring on the platform guard when his back was toward me and throw him over the rail, run down the steps and take to the water and strike out down stream and land below the picket line. All this looked possible, if done quickly and courageously. I knew the river was cold, but I thought that would be overcome largely by the great bodily strain that would be necessary to accomplish the desired aim. I was going to leave in my stocking feet, without coat or hat. Soon after the captain had gone, my captured pard's mother and aunt visited the prison. I had met the aunt in the country not far from Rome. I had but little to say and would not have said that if I had not been acquainted with "Aunty." The women were allowed full freedom and were not in any way restricted in talking, or required to in hearing of the guard, so the women stayed as long as they desired, and left at will. When they had gone, I beckoned my newly made acquaintance to one corner of the room and confidentially apprised him of my plans. He advised against such a hazardous effort as my chances of being shot down were many, if I did dispose of the platform guard, and if I succeeded in reaching the river, the mile or more in its waters that I would have to swim, would chill me to a helpless condition and that I would be drowned. I replied that I had no fear for the condition of my mind was such that determination had control, and as for drowning, I had long since heard it was one of the most pleasant endings; and it would happen out of sight and hearing of the enemy's hisses and scorns. When I was through, he said: "I know the captain better than you, as I have been here some days, and he has visited prison several times; I find that he is a great hand to have fun at the prisoners' expense, as I have heard him make threats before that he never carried out, but none so bad as yours." He said he was thoroughly satisfied that his intentions were to scare and he would get up some joke to tell his brother officers and he said he guessed he had, but it was hard on him and his man, for he did not think during life he had ever heard so much abuse as I had given those two men, and he was satisfied that the captain felt beat at his own game. He said some of the boys were telling the two lady visitors the happenings of the prison and they said: "We have just met the captain and he was telling us about it, and remarked that was the boldest and most daring man he ever had any experience with, but they knew there was no intent of his carrying out the threat as he was a nice gentleman and had visited their home several times." Later on, some of the other prisoners spoke of the matter in an encouraging way, and said: "Texas have no fears," when one of them laughingly said, "Substitute the word 'fear' with 'thought,' " and the party said, "I stand corrected." So the thing seemed to be as a huge joke on the Yanks and was being treated as such by my fellow prisoners, under the conditions. I soon gained my composure and reason—hope came to my relief and by night I had banished all idea of attempted escape. The captain paid us no more visits.

In this prison was the first and only time I ever had to take a dose of abuse of the Southern women. There was one of the platform guards one day who seemed to enjoy talking braggingly and roughly to the prisoners through the open door, and as the room was small, there was no chance to escape hearing his words, without stopping ears. This I had no inclination to do—I kept mum, but some of the boys would talk back, which was what the black-hearted wretch wanted. I had heard that such talk had been indulged in before, under similar conditions. He seemed to well understand where and how to reach man's sensitive point and to enjoy his helpless agony. When he was relieved, I said: "Boys, that was bitter; but remember the fellow either in war or peace, revenge would be sweet with me and I will be ever on the lookout," and during the war and years after peace there was no object so well photographed on my mind or vision as he. I think recognition would have been instantaneous. We were taken from prison, I think, the morning of the sixth day and marched to Kingston. My chum did not accompany us and I guess that mama and aunty had worked their influence. When we arrived at Kingston, my appetite had returned, to my great discomfort, for there was no provision made to relieve hunger. We spent the night and part of the next morning at Kingston and were forwarded by rail in a box car for Chattanooga, Tennessee. We had only one guard in the car and he was of the rank of sergeant and was armed with a Colt's six-shooter. He left one door open and stood in and near same. The train moved slow and at times was detained on sidings. From appearance, near the track, one would suppose there were enough soldiers near Sherman's front to quickly fill any gap the Rebs might make, and all seemed to be fat and well fed. If we had just destroyed great mileage of their transportation facilities!

When we took the car at Kingston, my ideas were set on jumping from the moving train at night and making my escape. I had said nothing to anyone about it, as I wanted no advice. During the day, at one of our stops, there was a handcuffed prisoner put into the car. My prison-made acquaintance was soon in conversation with him. I had gotten reasonably well acquainted with the guard, considering the short time. I found him very nice and pleasant of expression and asked him the cause of the prisoner's handcuffs. He said he was a noted "Gorilla," and he and his band was a terror and had murdered quite a number of their men, and it was said he would be shot—for the proof was sufficient. My sympathy was aroused at once for the prisoner, but I made no hint of the same to the sergeant, so when my prison acquaintance had left the handcuffed man and gone to another part of the car, I had a talk with him and he had his sympathy greatly aroused; said he knew the man and his name was Allen, and was known of late as Captain Allen and was the supposed leader of quite a lot of the natives who were giving the Yanks a good deal of concern and it was his and Allen's opinion, that he would be roughly treated and probably shot. He said he knew him as a quiet and industrious man up to the time the enemy put their invading foot on Georgia's soil; but since then, his nature seemed to have changed, and if reports were correct, he and his squad had been very successful and annoying; and that he had learned there had been a reward offered for his capture; so while together, we formulated a plan for the captain's escape in connection with ours, and as he was so thoroughly acquainted with the country, we would leave the point of the jump to his judgment. The plan was this: For each of us at times, singly or jointly, to stand near and fronting the door during daylight and for Allen to have but little, if any talk; and near the point of the jump at night, when we were advised the three of us were to be near the door and I was to be near the guard's side, conversing. The guard generally stood to the right hand of the door, leaning against or holding casing. Allen was to take middle position. All went well and our future looked bright, and we were at the post. When Allen jumped, I was to jerk the pistol out of guard's belt and jump or fall out, and if necessary, take the sergeant with me. The third man was to escape as soon as I cleared the car, and if I had carried the guard with me, he was near to render aid, if needed. The car was dimly lighted, and from side glances, unnoticed by the guard, I could see that Allen was under great strain. I now was fearful that he would break down and not take the plunge in the dark. I was two or three times nearly grabbing the pistol, thinking he was off. My anxiety at such times was so great that I was fearful the guard would, or had his suspicion aroused, but he did not. The train was making ten or fifteen miles an hour, and after standing in this condition a few miles all hopes were blasted. When we passed a line of low smoldering fires at right angles from the railroad and the guard remarked that it was our picket reserve, the idea flashed through my mind that we were in the city protection, and the reserve consisted of battle line. I asked how far to Chattanooga; and if I remember correctly, it was five miles out. About this time we were stopped and a reported block of track ahead. It was now well in the turn of the night. Pard and I stepped back and had a few words, to this effect: Day is about two hours off and in the enemy's line; speak to Allen and tell him to keep from near door, but if opportunity offers to slip out and under the car. The night was cold, and we fellows were chilled. The block ahead was reported bad, and possibly would not be cleared till day. We suggested to the guard the comforts of fire near the front of car door if he would permit Pard and I to get out, we would soon scrape up enough trash to get a comfortable warm fire. He consented. We were out and found ample fuel about forty feet from the track and soon had a bright and inviting blaze and were on the opposite side rubbing our hands and expressing the feeling of comfort and enjoyment. The rest of the boys were asleep, less Allen. We invited the guard to come out and partake of the comforts. He accepted and slid out of the door. Pard and I kept up a continuous talk. When the guard was near the fire, Allen slipped out and went under the car and had just passed from sight on the opposite side when the guard turned facing the car and stood for a moment, then went to the car door and looked in. He pulled up and scanned the inside, and then dropped to the ground, drew and cocked his pistol and told us to get back in the car damned quick. We sure got a move on us, feeling good of our success. The guard abused and threatened Pard considerable, but said not a word to me as he wholly blamed him and said he had noticed the intimacy between them several times. I have often thought what kind of a yarn the guard made, in excuse of his not being able to deliver Allen—the one the Yanks would rather have had than the rest of the bunch. I learned in a few days that their cavalry had scoured the near country thoroughly for Captain Allen, but had failed to recapture. We got into town after daylight, and were put in prison. The enclosure was a space about two hundred feet square and was enclosed by high brick walls. In this enclosure there was a single story house about thirty by one hundred feet, which had a brick or concrete floor and two barred windows on the street end. There was a shallow sink in the enclosure about three by ten feet and the stench from it was very offensive. I guess disinfectants were not known in those days, and as for brooms, if needed, one could use the frazzled end of a blanket. There was no vessel that one could have washed a garment in, if he was so lucky as to have a change.

There was no pretense of any offer by the captors of anything to aid or better the sanitary conditions. The accommodations were well crowded and when all were lying down, the floor of the house was fairly well covered; and I guess it was well it was so, for there was no provision made for heating and the weather at times was cold; but we all knew how to lie hog in the bed style and generally passed the night fairly well, for we had not over eaten and our conscience was clear—we knew we had committed no wrong, for self-preservation born in man is one of his strongest traits, and if killing an invader in one's country is not self-preservation, please define. We received a small amount of fuel daily for fires in the yard, but the amount was so small that it was rather a punishment, of a cold day, to the most of us, as half a dozen small Indian fires were about the limit—and that only for one burning. Fortunately for me and a lot of other hardened sinners who were there, we had roughed it so long that fire could be well dispensed with, only in extreme cases. Our daily rations consisted of a small thin slice of poor Southern milch cow, without any semblance of fat, and two crackers 3½ inches square by ⅜ inch thick. This was only issued once a day, and that a short time after daylight; but, oh, yea gods what a feast! After this sumptuous breakfast was served and before the good taste had gotten out of a fellow's mouth, there were a half dozen or more slick Yanks in the pen, getting laborers to work on breastworks near the city limits, and there seemed to be a combination or trust with them, for the price offered day after day was the same, and that was for six hours' work—on returning, as entering gate of the prison, to issue rations, same as breakfast. Some of the members of this labor agency were silver tongued and seductive and would always get a good force of weaklings. The Yanks were good paymasters, as I heard no accusation of sharp practice. I asked some of the boys who lived in the Sherman invaded section if they were not working for a small slice of Mama's milch cow and possibly had not the old lady assisted in threshing the wheat that made the crackers? There were, however, a large percentage of the inmates who had heads that controlled stomachs, and would refuse the agents with a vim. I told them that I would starve, die and go to heaven before I would help the Yanks, for I knew there was where a fellow would go after death if he left this earth, and there was no fear of hell with me, when dead; for the Yanks had changed the order of things by stealing or buying hell out and moving it on top down South, and I guess the trade was closed and Sherman knew what he was talking about, when he said: "War is hell." I think that my time in this prison was about fifteen days. I felt the pangs of hunger some, but not so much as one would suppose. I was daily looking around for a place to escape—the two barred windows looked most favorable. I knew my body was shrinking and would soon be small enough to at least give it a trial of forcing through. The head I tried several times, but it was not shrinking and was too hard to flatten. I envied some of the prisoners' small stature and head, for a size or two smaller would have surely worked, for the bars were openly spaced. The prisoners did not seem to worry much for the amount of dirt they wore. I guess it had more effect on the new beginner, for rags and dirt were no stranger to the old stager.

I had heard of the abuses the enemy were heaping on the South about the treatment of prisoners, and as I was an inmate of one of their prisons, I thought I could fairly reason on prison life, at least during the war; and I concluded that neither side had anything to boast of—for I assure the reader if the Southern prisons could beat the Chattanooga Yankee prison in filth, poor and scanty food, without fuel or heat, then at least they should give the South credit for being the most resourceful and ingenious, for it would have surely taken a genius to beat the Chattanooga prison, even with that to look at—for the rack and stake of centuries passed were not more brutal than the confinement in the cold, slowly but surely starving. I do not pretend to say that the Southern prisons were any better, for I never visited one to see; but I concluded they could be no worse. But thought would dwell on this one in particular, and that was: "Do two wrongs make one right: and is there no way yet devised to correct without fighting, as it were, the devil with fire," for the North surely was trying to correct the wrongs and abuses of the South and in doing so, was at least trying to place the North in the world's light as being more humane than the South. But when it comes to cold facts, such was not the case—it was not from any sympathy they had with the slave. Political supremacy was their aim, and could it only have been accomplished by making all the states slave holders, they would have whipped the South if they had opposed it, and claimed a monopoly on the negro privilege.

As I have stated before, my generation was one of warriors—made so by the preachers and politicians. The North was arousing the masses for political purposes and was wedding church and state for that purpose; and was teaching the young to look upon a Southerner in the light of the devil's emissary. The education of the South emanated from the same source, but on different lines. It was to weld church and state together to combat a threatened foe whose object was to impoverish by liberality, property which, under the Constitution, was not prohibited. For, as I have stated, if done for humanity's sake, then there must have been considerable change in this country in a short period—or the founders of our government were of the brutal type, as was claimed of the Southerners, or they would have had it provided for in the formation of the government. So, figuring as a whole, the responsible parties for the great flow of blood should not be laid at the Southerner's door, for the matter of property rights, as granted by the Constitution, should, at least be proof enough to exonerate; and the cloak of defense of preserving the Union was not the kernel in the nut—in my opinion it was to make a solid North and a solid South, and they knew they had us buried, politically; and as to the fighters—I at an early date thought it best to shake hands and quit, for we never had any quarrel, but the other fellow did.

When we heard of General Hood's entrance into Tennessee, my hopes of early freedom were joyful. I felt that we would be run North by train for safe keeping. My determination was: No more confidence, and sympathize with none, look out for self, and jump, regardless of risk to person, at opportune time.

I saw in prison, at two separate times, a Yankee in soldier's uniform, hanged by the thumb against the cook house wall. This was done by tying thumbs together and putting the subject back to the wall, raising the arms over his head, lifting the man a little and putting the thumb string over a peg, letting the feet barely touch the ground; and I think the torture depicted by the face, it must be a horrible punishment; and one cannot stand a great while before his head drops forward and to one side in great agony. They were both what might be termed young men and not of a criminal appearance—we knew nothing of their offense. I did not watch and see the finality; but one of them who was hanged near dark, was reported beyond reviving, when cut down—in fact was dead and stiff. This was done near our meat barrels. These barrels were for holding our boiled beef after it had been cooked and cooled and cut for issuing. I guess this meat was kept on exhibition and just out of our reach to aggravate our hunger, and it surely did, as I have stood and gazed on it, and often wished that I could get a fill of the sweet stuff. The sight of it would naturally have turned any stomach but a starving one—the way it was handled, and the lack of fat— and as the weather was cold there was generally several days' rations ahead. I think it was the next morning after we heard of Hood's rear move that we were ordered to get ready and fall in line. We were moved by the lunch stand and handed six crackers and three small pieces of beef, or its equivalent in one piece, and were told that it was three days' rations. I commenced storing mine away at once—not in haversack, however. We were ordered to march in double file—the guard had told us we were to take the train. We were marched several hundred yards to standing box cars. By this time my haversack was empty, and my stomach was not full. We were ordered to climb in, and with the help of a push-up, the cars were soon loaded. I had gotten well to the front of the column, and when we were at the first car and ordered to load up, I made myself useful in helping the boys up. When the first car was loaded, I had learned the number packed in. We were moved forward to the second car. I still continued helping, and when the count was in, we moved to the third—I was the last man in. I did this loading for two purposes: first to see arrangement of seating and the number of stowaways. The seats were made of one by twelve across the cars, from door to end, and were close together, and were loaded by walking over the top and each fellow stepping down, the short leg having the advantage as he would not be forced to cram his knees against the front seat. There were two planks with edges joining or double seat in the center, running lengthwise. This gave good space in front of the doors. This seat was for the guard, who was last in, and numbered five or six. When helping to load, my remarks were pleasant and catchy as I could make them. I was not playing for prisoners' favoritism, but for guards'. This I succeeded in gaining. The guard was just on the outside of our line, when loading, and could see all that was going on; and as the near ones would hear the words spoken, I was sure I was being heard and noticed. I took a seat on the guards' seat, facing, so in traveling I could be looking south. When the guard came in, there was one seated on each side of me and we were soon in conversation. I talked independently, but in a respectful and pleasant way. They seemed to be interested in my talk and asked a good many questions, and I did likewise. They were all natives and in their conversation well respected the feelings of the hearers. This was found to be the case in nearly all instances with the native born; but the fellow who was from the other side was generally coarse and crude; and nearly devoid of respect for those they were fighting; but this class of men at all times need sympathy, but made to fear law; as they have no make-up for respect or love for anything but brutal force. Before we pulled out, there was a surplus of guards, so claimed, and they were ordered in our car, until our guard number was nine. The first guard grumbled about being crowded, but never once said "move" to me, and kept on conversing—and the extra guards had to seat themselves as best they could. We moved out with both car doors open, and ran that way for some time, but the weather turned cold and drizzly and the north door, or the one to my back, was closed. We traveled some time this way, and the guards opened their well filled haversacks and commenced eating. I looked straight to the front to see other diversions, as a hungry man, having a middle seat at a feast, with no thought of partaking, has an indescribable feeling. The guard to my left, before he commenced eating, had sliced off a nice piece of fat meat and placed it on a cracker and offered it to me. I thanked him and took it—tried to be genteel in eating it, but my dog organ predominated to such an extent that I soon had the lot gulped down and was thinking of a story I had heard when I was a boy, of a plan that an old slave owner adopted to make his bacon hold out, and that was: To tie a string to a piece that could be swallowed and have his little negroes swallow and pull back, until they had gotten their full of fat meat. The right hand guard was not one of the sort to be beaten, so he soon had a duplicate in my hand, and I was equally as profuse in thanks and soon had it stowed away. I never was much of a talker while eating, and I assure you that I was not at this feast. When I got through, I felt good and said: "Boys, you are the right sort; and if you ever get out of this scrap and come to Texas, look me up, as I surely will be there and will see that you get a pleasant reception." One of them said: "Suppose you don't get out of the scrap, as you call it." I replied: "Have no fear, for I was not made to be killed by a Yankee bullet." They laughed and promised to call. The man who was sitting just behind and to my right, I think, had the Texas fever—for I had not much more than gotten through inviting the boys down, when he had a duplicate order to my front. I accepted, looked around and thanked him, and said: "Pard, I want to see your face so that I will know you; and when you come to my country I will tell the boys to treat you white." He thanked me. Now, each of these hand-outs was more nutritious than a day's rations. I sat and figured up the contents of stomach, which were: nine crackers, three slices of poor beef, three slices of nice fat, sweet bacon.

It finally grew dark, and my door of escape was yet open. The night was dark; drizzly and breezy. I was screwing up my mind to the jumping pitch and would think of Captain Allen now and then, and was suffering some of the agonies he had experienced. My chances were less favorable on account of the darkness, rocky conditions, as I supposed, and the number of trestles we were passing and a faster speed of travel. I was not as far in Tennessee yet, as I wanted to be when I jumped, so I did not take the opportunities as they were offered. We stopped now and then on sidings or at stations—at one of these an officer passed by the side of the car, ordering all doors closed, and stated that one fellow had dropped or fallen out at the back station. There was one of the guards, who sat on the front cross seat, with his right side leaning against the car with his legs stretched out, partly covering the door opening and the door closed toward him. The door was closed as ordered. The train started up, and there I was in a pen, as it were, with all avenues of escape shut off. One can imagine how I felt. We had gone but a short distance, when I discovered that the door would work open, but the guard with his legs stretched in front of crack would reach up and pull it to, when it would open a few inches. It was now well in the turn of the night, and the guard was sleepy and nodding, but kept the door in mind, but let it open a little wider at each time. I, at each opening—which was enough to force myself out sideways—would take the cowardly dread of falling out in a cut and bounding back, or dropping off of a high trestle. I had my blankets folded and on each shoulder, crossed fore and after; and U.S. belt around and fastened to my waist; my rubber cloth was in place with head through hole; hat was off and pushed between my body and the blankets—these were my earthly holdings. The guard was nodding nicely. When within about six or eight miles of Murfreesboro, Tennessee, the door was open enough to quickly force myself out sideways—the guard's left leg was so stretched it had to catch my full force at quite a disadvantage, and possibly a dislocated knee joint. My near associates were all dozing; in fact, I guess I was the only wide awake man in the car, although I was acting as though I was dozing. The car door was about twelve inches open; I arose, put my left foot on the guard's leg, just above the knee—sprang through the opening with my right side, giving door a shove. As I went, the train was running about fifteen miles an hour, and I could see light enough in front to know I would light in an opening and not in a deep cut—as I wished to avoid any chance of being ground up by the train. Up to this time I had a fair amount of practical test of mind working, but never before, or since, have I had this one opportunity.

After jumping, or falling, there was a light red or pinkish glow before or in my eyes—it was an instantaneous wave as a dim flash of lightning. I stopped walking, and my words were sounding, "A free man, by God," and to this day I do not know which was first—sight, word or act, or were they all one and the same. When reason returned, I was standing two or three hundred yards from the railroad track, facing the same, for just then a train passed. I was in a woods road and could see, in the twilight on each side, brush that indicated wood chopping. I was on the opposite side of the railroad from the side I had jumped, as I afterward learned. How long I had been in this dazed condition or how far I had walked, I had no knowledge. My rubber cloth was gone. I had a good sized lump on top of my head, and neck felt like it had been driven up. Neck and head soon became sore, although I had but little pain. I turned in the road and saw a wood pile near by to my right and front, and walked forward. I thought my course, to get out, should be southwest. I did not go far before day overtook me. I was on top of a high hill covered with cedar growth; was fairly well concealed from the surrounding country. The weather was cold, cloudy and wet. I could see about half a mile off, the railroad and one block house some distance down the track and sentinels walking the track to keep warm. I saw all was safe as I expected no hill explorers on account of bad weather. I crawled under a well spread cedar bush, rolled up in my blankets and slept a short time. I then crawled out and doubled my blankets over a cord and used them as a cloak or cape—the lower edge struck me near the knees. I was well wrapped, and as I thought there was no danger, I would take a stroll on the opposite side of the hill from the railroad. Only went a short distance when I discovered a log cabin on the hillside. I advanced and saw it was not inhabited. I found some dry leaf tobacco on stalks; stripped off a fair supply and was soon chewing a cud. There was a small amount of hay in the house and it looked inviting as a pallet, but was a risky place to sleep; saw the floor was loose. I raised a plank and pushed some hay underneath; put plank back and arranged hay to avoid detection; went out and crawled under and bedded up like a hog. There were all the comforts one could ask and just as I was dozing and thinking of sweet sleep, I heard the sound of horse's hoofs and a rider passed near the house. I saw he was not a soldier, but concluded I was taking too great a chance, so I crawled out and was soon up at my old place where the little snow, and wind was nearly a bar to visitors. I did not go to bed any more, but stamped around to keep warm until dark came. I could well scan the country for some distance from my elevated position and was carefully taking in conditions. Off about three-fourths of a mile from the railroad stood a small house—it was nearly one-half a mile from me. I could see from the chimney smoke that it was inhabited. It stood in a good sized open space, with but few small outhouses. I could see no one about, and concluded it was occupied by an old man and woman, and as the day was raw they were keeping housed. When night came on, I went forward slowly, not wanting to make my approach until the neighbors were housed. When I got within about two hundred yards I stopped until a time arrived that suited to my ideas, and when it did, I went to the front gate, which was about one hundred feet from the house and halloaed "Hello." I could see through cracks that fire was burning brightly. There was a reply through the crack, asking what I wanted. I asked the man to step to the gate. He said: "If you want to see me, come in." I replied: "All right," and went in, and made my presence known by tapping on the door and speaking. The reply was, "If you want to see me, you must come in the back door." I said: "All right, for I will be damned if I am afraid of you if you are of me." When I reached the rear of the house, I saw the door was open and what I took to be the kitchen opposite, but a few feet off, with a platform connecting the two doors. The platform was narrow—only about the width of the door, and when I stepped up I was nearly in front of the door. I saw my predicament at a glance. My plans flashed through my mind at lightning speed—how I ever thought and carried out a plan as though I had rehearsed it a number of times, I cannot tell. As I faced the door, with a bright fire-lit room about sixteen feet square, there sat my old imaginary man in one corner, near the fire place, and the old woman near the corner nearest me, but more in front of the fire. Near the front wall sat three men, and well back, near the center of the room, sat two more. They had on Yankee uniforms—I saw no arms. My first words, spoken in a commanding voice, were: "Are you soldiers." There was a chorus of voices, "No." I said, "I will not have you molested, then," and stepped in. My blankets stood well out behind, and U.S. buckle was very prominent in front, so they could not tell whether there was one or more six-shooters hung on. By this time the old lady was on her feet, facing me. I advanced saying: "Madam, I want some food for myself and three others; we were out scouting in front of Hood's army and last night we laid down for rest, and left no one to guard; and our horses and saddles were stolen and we are very hungry." She said she had nothing cooked. I said, "Go and see if you have none; bring a good piece of bacon." She rather demurred. I said: "Madam, I look rough, but am a gentleman—don't force me to act rude; go along." She started. My hat brim well shaded my eyes, so I could glance about, with but little notice. I turned my back to the fire and stood near the hearth, and threw my right hand gently to my back under my blanket, but not hard enough to rattle pistol. I was talking to the old man instantly, after getting the old lady started. I talked fast and commanding; told him we had not seen sun, moon or stars in the last three days and were lost, and I wanted direction. Asked how far to Murfreesboro. He said, "About eight miles." Asked the direction—he sulked. I said: "Old man, we propose no harm; don't expect to fire a gun while getting out, unless in self defense, but you must answer me; and if the answers are found not correct, you will suffer; if correct, you will hear no more of us. I expect to leave the three outer guards here for a time after leaving, and I advise all to keep indoors, so answer my question." He answered. I asked: "What direction is south;" he pointed. I asked the direction of the railroad—he spoke and pointed; asked how about the block house, guards, and such like, and he freely answered all, and some I knew to be correct; and from his precision and earnestness I felt they all were. During this time I was casting glances at the Yanks and four of them were swallowing it all; but the low, dark-skinned, heavy set center floor man nearest the back door had all the time exhibited a countenance of doubt. While I was putting questions to the old man he got up and walked to the kitchen. I caught myself in the act of ordering him back; he soon returned and sat down—I was looking for play. About this time the old lady came in with three nice slices of cold fried bacon, nearly a whole corn meal dodger, bottom of plate flowing with gravy or grease, and knife and fork. She stepped to the table near the door and placed it down, saying: "Draw that chair up and eat," meaning the one near me, that she had been occupying. I advanced, remarking: "I could eat it all, but the other boys are hungry and a divide will put us to the next chance." I thanked her. While I was talking, I had taken the bread in one hand and forked meat on top with my thumb to hold, gave a wishful glance at the gravy, and said good night to all, but "Don't leave the house for some time."

When I struck a dark place, you can bet I felt relieved, and was soon on my stomach with my head near a water hole about two hundred yards out, eating and drinking. I was near the path the Yanks would travel in going to the block house, but I had no fear of them, as I supposed the most skeptical one had accepted—as the knife and fork and gravy game was not bit at. From the information I gained from the old man, it dawned on my mind that I had crossed the railroad track in my dazed ramble, so I made my way across the railroad at a point of safety. From daylight observation, I knew the Yanks would keep well housed and they had no intimation of my routing, so I guess I was across the road and out some distance before they could give the alarm, if any. I trudged on that night, rather circuitous, keeping about what I supposed eight miles out from Murfreesboro. I would chuckle to myself now and then about the good luck I was having leaving Chattanooga—six rations going to and on car by prison reckoning, and the next day night, four meals, as reckoned by the old lady. I was very cautious that night and did not make any great distance, as I would avoid all roads and would not pass near a house, but I kept well the intended course if I did not have the moon or stars to guide me. The next morning about day I scanned the surroundings; saw they were good, and a house a few hundred yards off in a valley; the cedar ridge I was then on about half circled the place to the rear. I went down to the house, struck the back yard fence, and was near a lot. There was a fine lot of fat meat hogs in it. The place looked prosperous, and I could have bet and won that the owner was a Union man, and had not been foraged out by the Yanks. The public road was just in front of the house, but as the weather was yet rough, I had but little fear of Yanks being out on the bum that early. The man saw me; he looked to be fifty odd years old. He met me at the fence, apparently much excited. I had my little speech by heart, and it was: "There are three of us; the other two are on the hill (pointing the direction) and we are hungry, and want something to

eat." This seemed to excite him more, and he said he had
nothing. The dwelling had a hall through it, and in it I could
see what I thought to be a safe or cupboard. My reply was:
"You look to be in too good circumstances to make me believe that; and I insist that you at once go and get food for
three men. I do not wish to disturb your family, as I guess
they are yet in bed, but food I will have, and that in short
order. See that cupboard in the hall? I bet it has lots of goodies in it—move in a hurry. What do you say?" "I will go."
He soon returned with a good sized piece of corn bread and
a boiled hock of a good sized ham. I thanked him and said:
"We will stay up on that hill today, in the cedars (pointing
the direction) and would ask that you do not mention us if
the Yanks should come your way." He promised. I left, but
did not hide out in the direction pointed. I passed the day
not a great way from the house, under a well spread cedar. I
gathered up a lot of old field grass and bedded well against
the cold, wet ground. When I was well tucked under my
covering, head and all, I commenced eating. I was not long
at the job, and went to sleep, sucking the bone. I guess I
must have slept on my right side, without moving, as the
bone was in my mouth when I woke up. I had often heard
that snow would not quench thirst, but had never given it
any credit—here I had all the opportunities to make a fair
and extended test. When I awoke I was very thirsty, and when
I raised the covering from my head, I saw I was well snowed
under. I commenced eating snow, believing that it would
quench thirst. I soon found it did not. How I wished for a
tin cup to fill with snow and tuck it under the cover and see
if it would melt; for I felt that I would chill soon after getting
from under the snow and I was afraid to exercise for fear of
being seen. I laid under the cover until thirst was near torture,

then I slipped out from under the blankets—the snow had quit falling, but the wind was cold and brisk. I soon found a sink where the snow had partly melted and I drank all I wanted. Looked around, saw I was safe, and got under the cover again. I soon found the warmth had about left my burrow. My body was chilled and my clothing in places was frozen. I laid there only a short while and thought if I did not get to exercising, I would freeze. The sun was supposed to be near setting. I hurriedly arose, shook the snow from the covering, got a string through the double and all was frozen stiff. I got it to about place on my back and pressed against a tree and got it to partly encircle the body. I struck a trot to house, with the determination to risk all danger. I stopped at the back yard fence where I had been in the morning. Darkness was now near. The man was in back yard and had seen me and was at the fence about the same time I was. I saw that he was excited. I made up my mind to tell him a true story, thinking I would arouse his sympathy and he would render me some aid. I soon found sympathy and fear did not work together—the more I explained the more scared he became, and was standing, a trembling, speechless man. When I saw this, I had no idea of attempting to house up for the night with such a man; and I knew his soul rejoiced, if he had one, when I turned to leave. I asked him several questions. He stood trembling and speechless. I finally asked if there were any Rebel sympathizers near. He raised his right arm and pointed to his right front. I asked "How far," and in a trembling tone, he said: "A mile." I turned and trotted the way I came. It was now nearly dark, and I did not have far to go, before I was out of sight and hearing. I turned in the direction pointed out, trotted through fields, climbed fences and was nearly to a house before I saw it. It was about three-fourths of a mile from my unsympathetic man. I went to the front door and knocked. There was no reply. Went around to the back of the house—was met near back door by a man and was invited in to the fire. I saw a short distance from the residence, before entering, kitchen with glowing fire burning and smelled the sweet odor of cooking food. I entered a room which was sixteen or eighteen feet square, with large open fire place, with good fire burning. I stepped to the side of door and had gotten the frozen string untied that went around my neck to hold the blankets in place. The blankets were just slipping down to the floor—a woman entered with a plate of steaming food in her hands. She spoke and smiled. I stepped out of my standing blankets, for they were yet frozen and stood like a barrel on end. I was asked to have a seat at the fire. When the lady spoke and smiled the reaction was so great from a cold and heartless man to a sweet and sympathetic smile of a being of the highest order, that I could not suppress a tear that I brushed off with a hand that had not felt soap and water for weeks. I felt at perfect ease, as I knew I was with friends. I took a seat at the fire—did not feel much discomfort from the cold, but had the shakes or rigors. I could not talk without my teeth chattering. There was soon a table well spread near the fire, with hot, steaming food and a pot of hot coffee. I was told it was hog-killing day, and I asked for no further proof, after seeing the nice steaming dishes on the table. The little woman sure got a move on, and I thought: you are too well fed to be hungry; but I guess it is I you are after. We were soon at table, but up to this day, I can not tell whether I was hoggish or not. I remember that I had two cups of strong hot coffee—something I had not tasted for some time. Supper over, I faced the fire; still kept up my shaking, and I suppose the man knew more about such things than I did, for he remarked he thought I would have warmed up after eating a hearty warm supper. By this time the table was cleared and the little woman was by the fire, hearing what was said. The man said he had some good brandy and would liked to have given me a drink at first, but they were continually being hounded by detectives and they were abused and robbed if they were reported as aiding in any way the Southern cause (the idea flashed through my mind, how cruel in one's country) but he would risk it, and would do it if he knew I was a detective, for it would be an act of relieving suffering humanity; as there was nothing deceptive in my shake, so "Let you be detective or rebel, you shall have a drink." The woman spoke encouragingly, and said I was all right, as she had been tried enough and was hard to fool. The thought occurred to me: How different are nature's laws—no two beings alike—here courage and sympathy to the extreme, with poverty and beggary as punishment, if detected; at the place I just left, cowardice to a degree of suffering and void of sympathy for human kind. I thought that each was acting most suited to their natural make-up. There was soon a good sized tumbler or drinking glass in hand half filled. I asked: "Is this not too much: I am not used to drink." The reply was, "No." I swallowed it down. In about fifteen minutes the man said: "You are, by odds, the worst chilled subject I ever saw, and asked if I felt any effects of the drink." I replied, "No." He said he knew enough would stop it, and soon had equally as much down me. This made the amount a large glass full. In the course of a few minutes the chill was off. He asked several times if I felt any ill effects of the brandy, and I replied, "No," and that my head did not even feel light or swim. I had not talked much up to this time, but the brandy at least loosened my tongue. I found they were somewhat acquainted with Terry's Rangers,* as they had been in that section and they knew a few of the members personally. I told them of my capture, escape, etc., and of my experience with the scared man. Was told he was of my name. I said: "I have relatives in Tennessee by both father and mother, but I am not hunting up relatives; and I guess it was my good luck that I did not get in with that fellow, for he would have had the pleasure of turning me over to the Yanks, for correction, a son of Thomas Fletcher, his elder brother." From what I heard father say, and the direction and distance from Murfreesboro, and given name, he was my uncle. I told father of the circumstance, after returning home, and he said that he was my uncle. I said I was glad I knew nothing of my kinfolks and asked father if they were all Union stock; but he had not been advised. I sent my compliments to uncle a few years since, by a Mr. Sanders who lived near Murfreesboro and was visiting his children at Beaumont, Texas. I requested that he cite the incident and tell the old man all was of the past, and if he ever came my way, to at least stop and shake.

It was now near 10 P.M., and lodging was mentioned. I was asked not to stop for the night or next day, as they could not safely stow me away—as they had a negro girl in the kitchen, and the Yankees got their information from the negroes. After they had explained conditions, I said: "If you will

* *Texas in the War 1861–1865*, edited by Colonel Harold Simpson, U.S.A.F., states on page 113, "The Rangers were mustered into the Confederate service at Houston on Sept. 9, 1861 by (Texas Ranger, Benjamin Franklin) Terry and (Texas governor) Thomas S. Lubbock. At Bowling Green, Kentucky, the Rangers were formally organized as the Eight Texas Cavalry Regiment, one of the hardest fighting cavalry units in the Civil War."

give me directions to a more friendly neighborhood, I will be there by day, if trotting will get me there." He said there was such a place twelve miles out but that there were so many lanes and turns in the road that he was fearful I could not make edge of it, to a doctor's—giving his name—during the night. I said: "I can, if you will slowly give directions and the nature of the country." He started at the front gate and was very minute in instructions. When he got through, he said: "Do you think you understand?" I replied: "Yes, but would like you to repeat." He went over the same route again in the same tone and nearly the same words. I said: "Your first was impressed in every particular." I arranged my blankets as a cloak and was ready to start. He said: "Take another drink of brandy; you will need it, for it is now clear and cold." I did so. It was now about eleven o'clock. After clearing the front gate, I struck a trot—sometimes fast, and at no time walking, unless wading a stream as there was none to be crossed over knee deep at the road, but there were foot crossings at each near road. These I did not use. The road seemed to be as plain and familiar as though I had traveled it for years—the farm houses near by lanes, woods, hills and streams—were all there and looked for, before reaching them. Next to my last turn was to be in one of Murfreesboro's main public roads, with residence and other houses about two or three hundred yards on the hill on the opposite side, that I could see in the twilight. When I landed in this road, all was familiar, but from some cause inexplicable, I turned to the right. I trotted, and when I was about the distance of the turnout, I commenced looking and increased my speed. I was soon at a bridge that spanned quite a stream. It now dawned on me that I turned to the right, when I should have turned to the left. I wheeled and struck a sweeping trot. Day was approaching. I had about retraced half my steps when the sole of one of my boots became loose from toe to heel. I tore a strip off of my blanket and hurriedly tied it to place. This soon worked loose; I tied it again and fastened the ends around my ankle; then it worked back to the instep, and from the noise it would make on the macadamized road, a clog dancer would have thought he was not in the kerflop class. It was a cold clear morning. I did not think any of the surrounding natives were awake, and I wanted them to sleep on until I found hiding. I cut the sole off near the heel and started with the inner sole under foot. It was soon loose from the uppers and I had always thought the boots were too large; but I guess I was mistaken, for the inner sole was not large enough to keep the side of my foot off the cold, hard ground. After the sole had turned back a few times and let the ball of my foot on the ground, I tore another strip and took a few turns around my foot and sole by pulling back the upper. This was an improvement and I trotted on. Day was now well on me and I was at the place of mistake—the house just out from the road, and all looked open and public. I trotted a few hundred yards beyond the house and turned to the right and climbed a pasture fence; went about three hundred yards from the road to a rocky hillside. I was four or five hundred yards from the house; found a crevice in a rock, about twenty or thirty feet long, three or four feet deep; looked around and did not think I had been seen. Jumped into the crevice, kicked some of the ice and snow away with my good boot; and soon was lying down rolled up in my blankets, with boots off, tucked in with my body to keep them from freezing. I was comfortably warm, when I laid down and was asleep almost instantly. I awoke when the sun was about an hour high and it was in the right place, though

I had not seen it for days. I was cold; very cold. I realized that I was nearly frozen; will said "move," but my right arm was the only member that obeyed, and that feebly; all others were stiff. Hope and determination, I guess, aroused and went into action instantly. My arm would give a little at every effort and they were made at quick time. I was not long in getting the right arm to bend enough to thrust it forward as one hitting with a fist. Speed increased and thrusts harder, and in a short time I had a well limbered right, from shoulder to tips of my finger. I gave a push from the side of the rock and changed my body. I punched and slapped until the next that moved was my right leg. I soon gave, at hip and knee joint; I got it so I could catch it by the ankle. I strained and twisted—the left side soon let up so I could set up; all parts were soon limbered. I got up, but soon sat down, as I was too much exposed. I soon had on my boot and soles, one tied up, but while I was doing this I kept in all manner of squirming motions and taking deep and quick breaths. I mashed my bedding up so I could carry it and was out of the crevice, taking chances of better quarters. I made off at the best speed my legs would carry me, and soon had them limbered up: was soon out of the pasture and making for a cedar thicket I saw ahead. I was soon in and about one-half mile from the crevice; saw an open place about fifty yards long. Dropped my blanket and trotted, ran and walked the balance of the day in what was soon a well worn path, and I have often thought if that fifty yards of well worn path was not one of the wonders of that neighborhood. The ground was not rocky and did not pack hard, and I gave it a trial of speed in all gaits a number of times. During the day, with the sunshine and the breeze, my blankets dried and limbered up ready for use. I was now in something less than a mile of the doctor's—that I had started for the night before—so, in due time I called, spent a very pleasant evening, had a nice, warm supper and got fairly well posted. He advised that I go on a short distance and I would find a pen partly filled with seed cotton. I did so. When I got in the cotton pen, I felt at home and my mind was carried back to my early boyhood days, so I was not at a loss of knowing how to proceed. I soon had a hole scratched out and with feet and most of my body well covered, with blankets over my shoulders, I only had a minute of sweet anticipation of comfort, before I was asleep. I was awakened the next morning after sun-up by several large fat hogs that were making a noise of recognition of their owner's presence to feed them. I felt so comfortable that I hated to get up; but the thought of a good hot breakfast soon had me out. I thanked the owner for the night's accommodation; was asked to breakfast; found he had a large family, chiefly of girls, but all seemed neat and well kept. After eating a hearty breakfast, he said I had best move on and he would accompany me to near a house some distance off and then I could lay in the woods until night, then go up—the man was a shoemaker, and he thought he would make me a pair of shoes. I laid around in sight of the house until dark, and went up; found man, wife, and child. I was well received and treated. It seemed that the custom of the country was to supper after dark. This gave them an all day's work. This had been once a well to do country and all seemed to be industrious and not dependent on the negro slave. Their best horses were all gone and nearly all of their cow stock, and there was a great absence of milk and butter. The most of the inhabitants had a few fowl and hogs, and they seemed to know how to get good results. The man and I were sitting by the fire talking, and the wife was busy with her supper, when in stepped an evening caller—he was a doctor, past middle age, rather portly and jovial; rather inquisitive and pointed in his questions for a new acquaintance, and I used my tact to evade answers, and put up a nice little story to shield my identity. The proprietor finally burst out in a laugh and said: "Doc, you have found your match," and "Fletcher, you need have no fear, for he is one of us." All seemed to enjoy the turn of affairs, and I said, "Doc, a man in my business should be well versed in lying, and use it without blushing when conditions demand." We were soon acquainted and the old doctor was very companionable; and I learned he and his two daughters were residents of Murfreesboro, but had taken to the country on account of abuses, mostly by Yankee restrictions. Supper was announced and as the doctor had eaten, he did not go in. We had a bountiful supply and I thought the lady was as good a guesser as the one I had met two evenings before, or my natural appearance showed hunger. After supper we returned to the sitting room and it was evident that the doctor had not been idle; he lived near by and had been home and had returned with his two daughters—the younger was budding into womanhood and the other was a few years older. When I received an introduction I did not hang my head and blush on account of my unkempt appearance—in fact, I guess at the time that I made no note of it, as I was well trained to not allow clothing to be a bar to evening callers. The only article of necessity that I thought I needed was shoes and the landlord and I were understood on that point, as he had the material and was going to devote the next day and part of the night, if necessary, to make me a pair, and possibly after taking measurements, he had a pair under construction. I told him that anything would fit my foot that was large enough. The young ladies showed good common sense and were free to talk and did not seem to be inspecting me closely to get up a giggle; nor did they speak words of sympathy. They acted the true definition of friendship, which is: "He who comes in when the world goes out." After they had well looked me over they made their mission known which was to get me, as they said, much needed clothes. The older one knew of a good coat a few miles off that she would ride out and get the next day; the younger made several suggestions of places of probable finds. I said: "Anything will fit that is large enough." They laughed, and said the man of the house (calling his name) was safe as he was too small and would not I look funny in papa's clothes? They had mentioned over all the different items that I needed, including underclothes. When they got through I expressed my appreciation and said, "You can leave off underclothes and socks, as that is asking too much." They soon gave me to understand that they had my order booked. The mistress was seated with a three year old on her lap. Our talk now was in a general way, and about ten o'clock the doctor said: "Girls, it is time to go, as you and the shoemaker will have a busy time tomorrow." It was understood that I was to pass the coming day on a nearby hill that was well grown up with brush and I would have my dinner sent from the doctor's. I said that they need not trouble about dinner, as two meals were more than I had been accustomed to for a long time. In parting the young ladies said: "You will see what we can do by tomorrow night," and went off chatting, as though they were to perform the most pleasant duty of their lives. It was bed-time at our house also. I was taken into a side room—there was a nice clean bed that looked tempting, but the thought of my filthy person made me demur, and I said: "My blankets and the kitchen floor are good enough for me and better than I have been used to." The woman must have heard what I said—was soon on the scene and insisted; and said she did her own washing and ironing; and she would rather bed and cook for any number of dirty Rebs than the cleanest Yank in the world. I accepted and was soon asleep; had early breakfast and was soon in hiding. Saw no Yankees that day. About noon I was on watch for dinner—I saw the younger girl coming; she seemed to be well onto her job, as she scanned, every short distance, the surroundings. At the opportune time I stepped out into opening and was observed. I had a nice dinner and it was so plentiful that I easily left some. She said they had breakfast early and got sister off, and that she had returned, and named items procured; and the nice warm coat was one; and said that by night they would have me rigged out. Said her sister was doing the most of it, and papa and she were running the house. I asked her if she cooked dinner, and she replied, "Yes. Sister and I take it turn about, and do all the housework and sewing." I spoke approvingly of such true worth. After the meal she said she had enjoyed my company and would like to stay longer; but prudence demanded her presence at home as the Yanks might show up at any time, and papa and the Yanks did not get along well together. I remained in hiding until late in the evening, when one of my angels of mercy made her second visit with a message from papa, and that was, to come to the house as it was now so late that the Yanks would not be out that far, as they did not prowl out of their picket lines at night. I was met at the house by the doctor. He told me to go up stairs, and there I would find water, soap, and clothes. I did as bid, found the tub partly full of warm water—saw the clothes near by. I took a thorough scrubbing, head as well. When I got through, the water showed that most of the long worn dirt was off and my body companions, I guess, thought their time had come when I returned not to my cast off clothes. Before I got through dressing I thought there was quite a lot of life's valuable time lost in civil life in dressing once a day; and that the soldier had the one advantage at least of putting on and wearing off. My clothing consisted of full outfit. When I had gotten them on and hair combed, I felt "dudish," and when I smiled before a glass, I had the vain thought of "How handsome." I "primped," as the girls call it, before the glass quite a time and thought, as I think the most of them do, "Here goes to make a mash."

When I went down stairs the old doctor was near at hand, and as soon as he sighted me, laughed heartily, called the girls and they all made merry over my improved appearance. The doctor vouched for me being the same man who went up the stairs, as there was no chance of escape, as he had been near, all the time, to answer my call, if any—and he did not see how clothing could make such a change in appearance. I was well entertained that evening and did not demur at sight of a clean bed; had breakfast early the next morning. Before leaving, I asked that they deliver thanks to the shoemaker and wife for their kind treatment and the nice pair of shoes. I thanked the doctor and the young ladies profusely, and asked the doctor to keep up his good cheer if he was away from home. I struck across the country toward Franklin, hunting a man who was reported as once belonging to the Rangers, but had not left Tennessee with them. I inquired, as I went along, for him and soon got an appointment. I found from the different inquiries that Captain Van Houghten, as he was called, was a very important man to a large section of the country; and was a terror to evil doers. I had, up to this time, frowned on his mode of warfare and keeping law and order, thinking it would do more harm than good; but from observation and inquiry, the good effects over balanced the bad and should be more general in a country that is being invaded, for the opportunities are such that each army is well supplied with thieves and robbers, and some of them are enlisted; but of no service—plunder is their aim. Some are not enlisted, and rise up as if out of the ground, and uniform and at will pilfer their neighbors and it is almost invariably laid to the invaders, where in fact, outside of their well guarded confines they go in squads under an officer and take only as needed or instructed; and if it were not for such men as "Van" and a few scattered followers, the outlying districts would suffer more than they did; for they were the much dreaded of the wrong doer or criminal class, let them be from either side. I soon met Captain "Van" and found him to be a nice, courteous gentleman and not at his vocation for gain. He agreed to mount and arm me, but the horse was some distance off. At the appointed place and time I received a horse and equipment. The horse was only a loan, however, as he only had two and he often needed a change. But as our army was near, his territory would be more confined. I did not have to wait many days before I was in the saddle. During the time of the wait, I had supper at a house with some of Hood's advance. There was a fine looking young lady visitor who entertained the crowd while waiting for supper, on the piano. I did not go out to the first table, but remained in the parlor with two others. She asked our names and where we were from. When she heard my name and where from, she tried to rake up kinship for herself and the lady of the house. From what she said of Tennessee relatives and knowing that there were some of the same family in Texas, I thought we were second cousins, but at once thought of my scared uncle, and kept mum. Father claimed to be of Scotch-Irish descent, and this young lady showed Scotch-Irish blood. I guessed we were kin, but I had enough of the Fletcher stock at that time, and played ignorant.

It was about thirty-six hours after this that the battle of Franklin was fought. I was a few miles to the rear of the enemy's line, by my idea of location, from sound. The discharge of small arms was very distinct. I was lying near the house where I had passed the night and was to return for food and bedding the coming night. My place of hiding was a favorable one. It was a deep hollow, well grown up in bushes. I stayed close, as it was near a public road. The battle roared, and I knew that this was one battle that I would hear and not participate in. The whole day's fight, from my distant position, seemed to be stubborn, as neither side seemed to give. Along in the latter part of the evening the rabbits commenced passing me, and were passing when I left. There were hundreds of them that had drifted to that hollow and were going from the battle noises. I stayed at the house that night and found that there had been a regiment of Yankee cavalry camped near my hiding out place that night, which was less than one-fourth of a mile away. The next morning I received the horse. "Van" said he was trying to gather a company of young men and boys, and to go out with them, and wanted me to help him. This I promised to do. After receiving the horse and arms, I felt more comfortable and rode over the country considerably. I did not know what the army was doing, after the battle of Franklin, for after getting the mount, I kept out of harm's way, waiting "Van's" call; but I surely enjoyed the outing. One day near noon I was sitting on the gallery at the doctor's talking to the young ladies, and about half a mile to our front on a ridge, there put in an appearance a wagon train, and the way it was headed cast a gloom over my thoughts. The young ladies were very much exercised and were fearful it was leaving the country and that they again would be with the horrid Yankees. I thought their surmise was correct, but did not express myself, and tried to dissuade, for I could see depicted in their countenances the anticipated dread. I mentioned the possibility of the train being out on a foraging expedition, but I could see this did not quiet their fears. The old doctor was not at home, but I wished he were, for some hard words from him of abuse of the Yankees would have been a relief to me, as it would have been more suited to my nature and would have aroused hatred, but as it was, sympathy predominated. I cut my visit short and was on horse, riding off, thinking: "How noble is one, to love his country; how sad the fate to mingle with those you hate."

In the course of time Van Houghten informed me he had men gathered and he was ready for me. He said he had reported and was ordered to keep in the rear and flank, and to follow the army on retreat. We did this—sighted only a few of the enemy on the way out and had but little to do. The greatest trouble was something for man and horse to eat, and we seemed to have no connection with the supply train. Therefore, drew nothing. I was so hungry one morning when I struck where the infantry had camped for the night, I got down and threw some smoldering chunks together and had a fire started and threw on such bones and cows' heads as were handy to roast. The boys who had camped there had roasted the most of the bones once, but were not onto their job as well as one who had served a time in a Yankee prison; so I scraped and sucked hot bones until I appeased my hunger, and after that I had better luck in foraging. The Yanks were rather closely following our squad. One day, when we were at a stream, about one hundred feet wide and swimming—it seemed to be swollen by rain as it had the appearance of a ford—we saw a small boat at a landing. The recruits seemed to be excited and would not take to the water. I proposed to Van that he make a show and keep the Yanks back with two or three men, and I would get the boys across. He agreed. I ordered the boys to dismount and shove their horses in, when I swam my horse. I unsaddled and stripped, and sent a man over with my outfit in the small boat. The men were to cross in small boats after the horses were across. I rode in and slipped off my horse and swam it across; the most of the horses were pushed in but would not follow, so I returned and mounted another. All followed this time and the men were soon across. All was safe if we got away from the landing, over the hill. I hurriedly saddled and mounted, with my clothing in my arms and before me—the bullets by this time were coming near. There was a residence just on the top of the hill near the road, but I paid no heed to the lookers on and was too cold to blush. I dismounted at a safe distance with the rear guard out, and dressed. The water and wind were cold, and I guess would have been hard on a fellow unaccustomed to hardships. On this retreat I thought of Napoleon's disastrous retreat with bare and bleeding feet—here it was to be seen, now and then.

After crossing Tennessee River, I rested with the army two or three days and thought from what I could catch from "Van's" talk, that when he had his men assigned to some command, he would return; so I proposed to return him his horse, which I afterwards wished I had not done. I saddled up a mule one night, while not seen, and rode off. It was very cold and when I started I thought I would suffer, but such was not the case, as I had plenty of exercise to keep warm in getting the mule to go. I rode nearly all the next day, but stopped for the night. There was a man and wife at the house. They seemed well supplied with food for man and beast but the man was afraid he would not get any pay, and would, every little while, speak of being "eat out by soldiers." This I did not believe, as he had plenty and I saw that both I and my horse got plenty. He looked young and able enough to have been in service, but he was in such a hide-out place I guess the conscript officer could not find him, and as I had just passed a distillery in the hills, I guessed he was on the hide-out order—at least, after the war. He went over his liberality story again, while his wife was cooking breakfast and said he was done feeding without pay. I encouraged him in his determination, and told him he should have stopped it long ago; in fact, if the settlers had not started it, there would have been less stragglers, as the boys had plenty to eat in camp. But I never intimated that I was penniless; so he and his wife cheered up, he especially. After breakfast I saddled up and hitched at the front gate and went in, bade the lady good-bye and thanked her. In coming out, I passed the man standing at the fire place, gave him a hearty shake and thanked him. I was the only one who seemed to have the power of speech or motion in the house. I mounted and rode off in a path that was straight for two or more hundred yards. The man was motionless every time I turned my head and looked back. I enjoyed the scene and had a hearty laugh, and have often wondered what were his first words.

I traveled about twenty miles that day, in a rough country and took up at a small but well kept farm. The family consisted of man and wife, son and daughter. There was plenty of corn in the crib and the table was well supplied with corn bread, bacon and sour kraut; and I and my mule had a good appetite. I soon found the man was a trader and he made a proposition and I accepted it, but did not carry out my part in all particulars. He said he needed a farm mule and I needed a saddle horse, and said he had studied up a plan for each to get what he needed. I told him to out with his plan, as I was ready to mount at the first opportunity; that I had a long ride before me to reach my command, and possibly would have some trouble to get around Sherman's army, as I supposed the Rebs were still at the front. His plan was for me to steal his neighbor's three year old stallion—from his description, the colt was a bute, but too young for hard usage; although I kept mum on that point. His plan was, that when night came, he would go with me to near the place, which was one and one-half miles off. I was to ride the mule near to the house and unsaddle, then get horse out of the stable, saddle up and ride off that night. I told him I would study the matter over and let him know the next day; that I was too near worn out to travel at night unless I was forced to. He consented and said I could stay as long as I wanted if he could get the mule—I had already told him that I had no money. The next morning I told him it was all right,—with some changes. I was to remain three days and two nights longer and he was to keep the mule in the barn out of sight, so none of the neighbors in passing would see him, as they might recognize the mule after I had gone and he would at least be suspicioned of being a party to the colt's disappearance; and further, I would ride the mule to the place and when I got the horse I would return with the mule. He readily agreed to this. I and the mule had been fairly well treated up to this time, but the balance of my stay was made much more pleasant; the young lady was more talkative and pleasant, and "bud" did not hang around when the young lady and I were wishing the war was over. The old man kept the mule well housed and said he was currying him night and morning and soon would have a different looking animal of him. Time now passed rapidly and I wished I had set it twenty-four hours longer, for I had struck a bonanza—plenty to eat, comfortable bed and chairs, boy to make fires and man to feed and curry the mule, and a pleasant, quiet, good-looking woman for mother-in-law—if the girl said so after the war was over and I passed that way. I guess the old man would have readily agreed as he and I agreed so well, I would have been a handy fellow to have in the family. The time arrived —had early supper; my hostler had the mule curried and saddled and at the front gate. It was now dark and we had no fear of being seen, as there had not been a person passed that way during my stay. I was to get the horse and return and hitch the mule at the front gate, during the night. The old man gave me another recital of the roads and directions. I got a pleasant farewell, with many wishes of safety during the balance of the war, and to be sure and come by that way on my return to Texas. My last words were: "I am going to try to make quick work of this job and you keep a watch for mule." His reply was: "Nobody will see him hitched to the gate when daylight comes." I knew he was right in his prophecy. As I rode off, the thought came to my mind: who was the bigger liar and thief of the two—the one who received kind treatment and attention deceptively, or the one who planned to have his closest neighbor's only horse stolen? I passed near the house of the colt owner, as it was on my road in the proper direction. I went about eight miles that night and stopped at a house; traded the mule the next morning for a very good old saddle horse that I rode through to my command. I have often wondered if my man sat up all night or ever saw the mule afterwards; or did he ever learn that stealing was bad at best, and was it not a greater sin for two to steal than one.

I somewhat justified my act by the thought that he had contributed something to the support of the army, as he was well able to shoulder his gun and his family were such that they could make a comfortable living without his aid; so, if a straggling soldier did not tax him now and then, he would have been a useless citizen; and I guessed the assessor had not found him, and if he had, the little he would have gotten would not have been worth the ride.

On my way to my command I passed across the country that Sherman and Johnston went over on Sherman's advance to Atlanta, Georgia. The fencing had mostly been burned and some of the houses abandoned. I struck their line of devastation, so I could ride across it in one day, as I expected nothing for man or beast. While the whole day was not occupied in the line of contention of the two armies, the nearby country was closely foraged. I was told before entering that all I would see was women and children and a few old or crippled men; and that the mothers were walking long distances to get food for their children; which they brought in on sled drawn by two or three year old beef, which they butchered. I was also told that the continuous noise of the contending armies had driven all winged creatures from the country. Hearing the reports caused me to notice particularly, and in my hard days' ride I found things about as stated, for destitution was on every hand and to an extent one cannot well conceive, unless seen. But such is war, and yet at this stage of civilization and short period of emerging from the war, you will still hear men talk of war as though it were but a matter of killing off a few men and the satisfying of a few others by pension. They seem to have no thought of the suffering many, and I have learned that those who agitate war are mere trumpets and not fighters.

I got with my command in the Carolinas and they were still battling with the enemy and slowly giving to their pressure, but from what I could see we made no great resistance. My horse was not fit for duty when I reached the company and I and one other member of "E" obtained a permit to press horses. We started out and had some trouble in finding a mount, as the country had been well searched. On this trip we rode up to a fine residence, situated on an elevated point with a farm on three sides. The dwelling was a magnificent two-story structure and I thought at the time, it was the most beautiful residence property I had ever seen. We were met at the gate by an old man who said he was the owner of the farm. We told him our business. He said all of his best horses had been taken, but pointed to the edge of a field about one-fourth of a mile away and said if we would enter the woods at that point we would find several horses about one hundred and fifty yards in, in charge of an old negro man; said he had them hid there hoping that the Yankees would not find them, but that they were all old stock and only fit for farm use; but if we found any that suited, to take them, leaving ours instead. We went as directed and found the horses as represented. They showed good keeping and were at one time a fine lot of large horses. We saw nothing that we wanted and started to retrace our steps to the opening when we heard the firing of guns at or near the house. When we rode into the opening, we saw the house enveloped in smoke. We stood and looked on in awe but a few moments when the flames burst forth. My feelings I cannot describe at seeing the destruction of that beautiful house of an old and once wealthy family. I saw a rider coming our way and when he came up, he said there were four or five dead Yankees in the yard; that a squad of Rebs had ridden up on them when in the house, plundering and firing the same; that they were trying to force from the three women the whereabouts of their valuables. When they saw the Rebs, they ran for their horses which were hitched to the fence, and were all shot down. Our informant said the old man of the place was so enraged that he took a butcher knife and cut each man's throat. In a few days after, I understand there were two meetings under a flag of truce, directed by the enemy's cavalry commander and the Confederate cavalry commander. Reports said that the Yanks were much wrought up over finding their men with their throats cut and threatened retaliation at the first truce. General Wheeler investigated and reported the finding at the second truce; and stated that after the Yankee general had received and read his report, if he carried out his threat—that he held a far greater number of prisoners than he did, and that two for one would be shot, if retaliation was resorted to. I suppose the matter was dropped, as I heard nothing more of it, the second day out. Pard and I found a fairly good horse for each and returned to our command. We found the country well stocked with roving bands of both armies. I heard of one instance of dare-devil bravery which, if true, was nerve of the highest order. It was reported that one of the Rebs captured quite a squad of Yankee cavalrymen by secreting himself and when the front of the squad was opposite, he stepped out and commanded surrender or he, with leveled gun, would shoot commanding officer. It was said that the whole party shed their arms and stepped off at his command. I often thought if this game could be worked on well armed soldiers, the fellow who has robbed a stage coach or railroad car, in comparison, had not done much.

One of the most interesting sights to be seen in the campaigning of the Carolinas was the firing of the great mounds of rosin that were made from distilling of turpentine. The firing was said to have been done by the Yankees, and I guess to a great extent, true; but the old saying, "Give a dog a bad name, and you may as well kill him," was brought to mind, when I had to ride some distance above the road crossing to ford a lively stream that was covered some distance with burning pitch. I was alone, and was satisfied there was not a Yank in five miles when the mound was fired. One would often see the smoke of several of these fires in a day. The heat was so intense at the base that there would be a column of smoke nearly perpendicular, hundreds of feet high, where it was calm. When it struck an upper current of air, it would float with the breeze and would remind one of a great serpent crawling; and it could be seen miles away, and often more than one would be in sight. I had read of cities being plundered or sacked, and I had a desire to see it done, if one was ever so unfortunate, and I was near at hand. Columbia, South Carolina, was the unfortunate. The last day of the Confederate forces' evacuation, I was with a detail of about seventy-five men who were in the city to get clothing and such like for the command. We found but little, if any, but at one business house at which we were halted, the proprietor reported a lot of bottled imported gin that he would rather see us take than the Yankees. Some of the boys took two bottles, some one, and a small per centage touched not. I was one of the two-bottle crowd, and when we rode out of the city, I had a well filled bottle in each saddle pocket. The detail went

a short distance out of the city and were thrown in line fronting the river near a bridge. I think we were just above the
city. We remained in this position, sitting on our horses for
some time. The bridge was of good length and enclosed on
the sides. We had a few men on the opposite side of the
stream and there were some gun reports heard every short
while; and they gradually came closer, and now and then a
bullet would whiz near us. Soon a few scattering cavalrymen
would cross the bridge, coming to our side—the bridge
seemed to be well prepared for firing, for without any thought
on our part, the structure burst forth in smoke before the last
men at horses' speed passed through. There were two who
came onto the bridge together, and there was fear of their not
getting across; but it was reported they did, although they
were well scorched. The last and most gritty of the boys who
was near the enemy's front was either burned or checked. Just
as he came to the bridge the smoke was so dense from our
position we could not tell. It was reported that he perished.
Our detail was then abusing, to the fullest extent of words,
the cowardly act of the bridge firers for applying the torch so
soon. While in the line, I thought of my gin and opened a
bottle, and the most of the boys did the same. I was not used
to drink, but wanted to test gin as a fear tonic; so I partook
of the remedy freely, but the bullets would make about the
same impression at each visitation, and when we were
marched off, the most of one bottle was gone and the bullets
sounded the same old way. There was a detail made up while
we were moving to go back to the city, and see if it could
get any forage for our horses. I was not put on this detail,
and I said to one of the boys: "Let's go to the city tonight,
and have some fun." He said: "All right, if we can." I said:
"Play drunk, and follow me." He did so. I did not feel in

the least, any effects of my drinking, under excitement, but to all appearances, I was just able to set on my horse and when the detail filed off, Pard and I went with them. There was a protest from the officer, but we did not heed. When we struck the road that led to the city, there was a heavy guard to keep stragglers out, for they said the Yanks would take possession that night. The officer pointed out the two drunk men who did not belong to the detail, and the guard made an attempt to arrest us; but I told them that our horses were hungry and that Pard and I were going to feed them, if it was in town. The guard was infantry, and there was an officer present who seemed to have charge. They were now close up and around Pard, and I with the detail passed through. I put my hand on my six-shooter and said: "We are Texas boys; clear the way." The officer said: "Let the damn drunken fools go." So we were soon with the detail and got forage and remained in the city as long as we wanted; found a dozen or more cavalrymen on the same mission as ours, which was to take in the city, less that part where the enemy were shelling. They seemed to have been put onto the whereabouts of ammunition storage and they kept up a continuous thump at that point from their artillery—but it was said to have all been moved. Pard and I passed out where the guard was, about ten o'clock, but all were gone. We went about a mile further, rode off the road into the woods and camped; gave our horses a good feed and were up and riding back to the city early the next morning. When we arrived in the city, all was quiet; but it did not stay that way long. I had heard no talk of sacking the city that morning, or evening before; the enemy had not crossed the river and taken possession. In our rambles we struck a man who asked if we could use some cotton or woolen cards, as he did not want them to fall into

the hands of the Yankees. We accepted, as we knew something of their scarcity and value, so he gave each of us two
pair of cotton cards—one of my cards proved to be wool,
after it was too late to correct. By this time there were about
the same number of rebel stragglers that there were the evening before. From what I could see, however, they were all
good men, out of place, however, as the last one of us should
have been with our command. There were groups of the under grade of whites and some negroes gathering in the business center of the city. We had concluded to go out and I
guess the most of the other stragglers were of the same mind
for it was time for the Yanks to have laid their pontoons and
commenced crossing. Just as Pard and I had gotten through
the principal part of the mob, on our way out, we heard a
crash and a great confusion of voices behind. When we
looked, we saw all rushing for the point of the noise. We
turned and did likewise, and as far as I could see, the balance
of the straggling Rebs did the same. We found that a front
door of one of the fine dry goods houses had been forced and
the mob crowding in, so one after another front was burst
in. Some one of the straggling Rebs crowded his horse onto
the side walk and fired a few shots over the head of the surg-
ing mob inside and hollowed get out. From this, the mobs
in other stores were shot over and it was surely amusing. Men
and women were packed and grabbing—some had large pack-
ages on their shoulders; but when a shot was fired, all dropped
their goods, turned and made a rush for the door; and from
the way they jammed and piled, there must have been some
hurt. I only watched this performance a few minutes and rode
away, as it would have been a good place to have been captured. This was certainly a rough mob and they seemed to
have no regard for fine glass fronts; they would batter them

down, as if they had no value. How far they went with their plundering I do not know, for the first sight of the break and wild rush satisfied my curiosity, and I thought if the boys who were doing the shooting to frighten had only done it at some of the leaders, it would have had a better effect. Pard and I got a good dinner that day for the cotton and woolen cards, and the woman who furnished it thought she was fortunate, and said she had fed a good many Rebs that day and the cards were ample to pay for all, if one was woolen. One rarely sees cotton or woolen cards now, but they were a great factor during the war, and how the South would have kept clothed without them would have been a serious question, and would have added far greater suffering. I traded my pair of cotton cards for a good pair of pants and both the receiver of the pants and the cards were made happy.

After the evacuation of Columbia, the Rebs did not seem to be much in Sherman's way, for we seemed to be very much on the run. The Terry Rangers were moving one day, which was said to be only a few miles out from Raleigh, North Carolina, when the Yankee cavalry surprised them. This was my first experience of being with a body of surprised men at rest, but it was soon over, and the Yanks were on the run. It looked like some of the boys who did not saddle horses were expert bareback riders and were in the charge among the first and seemed to handle self and their horses with ease. The last time I was on the firing lines, was said to be near Bentonville, North Carolina. I was near Colonel Cook* of the Rangers when he was seriously injured. He was shot at long range, across an opening—just when this happened we were for-

* Lieutenant Colonel Gustave Cooke was commanding Terry's Rangers at this time.

warded in column some distance, in a sweeping lope, running into the Yanks who were near cutting us off from the bridge. I made an effort to make a large squad of the enemy surrender, by running to their front when they were double-quicking to their rear. I was about fifty yards to their front demanding, "Surrender," thinking they were cowed; but two shots from the bunch made me think they were not a surrendering lot, so I got out of the foolish scrape, scared but not hurt. After their two shots, I was satisfied they were onto their job and were running in mass to form hollow square to guard against cavalry charge, and were reserving their fire or they would, no doubt, have emptied my saddle. I have often thought, of all the simple acts of my life, this one headed the list, and it is noted among the unexplainable. After this, bullets seemed to make a greater noise than usual and one would hear, now and then, a word of discouragement as the men had been driven so much that there was a muttering of disapproval of those in authority of their mode of warfare. This was the first and only symptom of dissatisfaction that I ever heard.

Surrender and Return Home

＋══＋

WITH THE ARMISTICE of Johnston and Sherman, and report of Lee's surrender, all hopes were gone, and the thought of returning home, defeated, seemed to be depicted on each face, and for a few days I don't think I saw a smile, and there seemed to be a manufacturer of false reports near by. Some of the reports said we would all be sent North; others said we would be put in camp and held for months, so there seemed to be a mania for making up unfounded reports and the condition of one's mind was such that there were some of them taken seriously. As for myself, I think I passed a few days of the blankest part of my existence. I seemed to have no thought of the past, present or future. How long one's mind could have remained in the condition as I felt, without some order of transformation, or as it were, a changed man, I do not know. Fortunately, however, the spell was soon broken; and I awoke, as it were, to realize that there was a future. I have ever been thankful that during the war and since, I carried no hatred against the victorious foe: and I soon learned that they looked upon the cause of the strife as I did, and performed it as one of their most sacred duties. The incident that made me a reasoning being was very simple, and crude: but through life I have at least made it mind's comfort at times, when things did not go my way, by getting in the band wagon, as it were, and bend an influence and not stand off and curse and make matters worse.

Now for the incident. It was a few days after the armistice had been in force that the cavalry was moving at night and we were passing through a piece of woods in a well worn country road. At this point the road had been worn down considerably where passing over elevation, and there was not sufficient room for two columns, so it seemed that the infantry at that point was moving also and had given the road to the cavalry and were lying on the bank to our right. There was, as usual, some talking between the cavalry and the infantry. I was napping, or nodding, as it was near midnight, when I heard one of the cavalrymen a short distance ahead, ask what regiment was that. The reply was North Carolina Regiment, giving the number. Then the cavalry boys began to say "Tar Heel," when one of the Carolina boys drawled out, in rather a long tone: "Boys, have you got any bacon." The reply from the cavalrymen was: "Yes." The North Carolina man then said: "Grease and slide back into the Union." The remark and the novel way of the use of bacon, forced a laugh from several. I joined in and we were soon discussing the merits of the North Carolinian's advice. I laughed and thought, and had not ridden far before I made up my mind to follow the lesson taught by the crude advice; so from that I commenced to think of the coming civil life and day by day the sunshine of my being grew brighter.

In a few days there were about one hundred and fifty of us started for home, without permission or parole. We rode

out of the army lines at night—we had a lieutenant as commander, and passed over country in some places that knew
nothing of the ceasing of hostilities. At one small town we
passed, the town authorities opened quite a large storeroom
of army supplies of bolt cloth, and such like. The news of
the opening for the soldiers soon spread and the citizens gathered in considerable number—the soldiers went in, but got
little of any use. The most of the boys cut off pants patterns.
There was no attempt to close doors after the soldiers came
out, for by this time there was a jam of citizens who seemed
to want all they could get while the opportunity offered; so
they soon filled the house, which had a platform—and there
were some amusing incidents seen, both men and women
were in the grab; and when a fellow inside would shoulder
up a bolt of goods, his rights would soon be contested; therefore, there would be a scuffle and unrolling of the bolt with
a run for the streets and there was quite a piling up of those
who retained their hold too near the edge of the platform.
The whole street front was soon a struggling mass, with numbers of pocket knives being used to get a part of the bolt at
least; and in some instances the cut was very small. It was all
done in a good humored, noisy crowd, but the divide was
not an equal one, by any means. We soon rode off and I
guess the authorities shut the doors on an empty room. As
we rode out of town, we struck a fellow who had whiskey for
sale. I rode by his place and got my canteen filled, so with
others doing the same, we had plenty of whiskey for the squad
for all time, if they stuck to that brand. After I had taken a
drink and passed to those who wanted, I took the second
drink to see if it tasted as bad as the first—it did, and I soon
thought, from its quick-acting qualities, that I had not grown
rich from its effects, but sick. I soon felt too sick to live, but

not sick enough to die. I soon drew the stopper of my canteen and emptied it, and I thought after seeing its contents, of all the men in the world, that town had the meanest in that whiskey peddler and that he would be out of luck if he passed that way while I was so sick. I don't think that there was ever a greater amount of chewing tobacco used in whiskey, or I got the dregs of the barrel, for in emptying the canteen the mouth would nearly stop by pieces of cut plug tobacco.

We rode into camp after dark and this was my first and only time that I remember of failing to care for my horse. I managed to unsaddle him and pour corn on the ground. I made no attempt to spread blanket, as any place was acceptable. Sickness soon wore off, and I got a fairly good night's rest; but it was some time before I tried the "get rich quick" plan again. On this trip my horse had about given out and I asked the lieutenant for his consent for one of the other boys and I to remount, and I would see that the mount would give his command no trouble, as I was going to get it from the Rebs, who did not know the war was over and that all our army stock belonged to the Yanks. He consented and gave me directions of travel so I could catch up with the squad. So the next day, just before noon, we passed through quite a town and I told the officer that I would drop out near the outskirts. When we passed through, there were quite a number of government teams parked near where we entered the town. The squad only halted a short time in town to inquire the way, but said nothing of Lee's surrender, or Johnston's and Sherman's armistice. It looks strange, in this day of progress, that not so many years hence, the news of so important an incident traveled so slowly in a well settled country; but such was the condition then; for we traveled some distance before the news that hostilities had ceased, was known. After passing through the town about half a mile, Pard and I turned to our left and rode off the road about two hundred yards, unsaddled and rested the balance of the day near a small stream of water. Near night there were two fine four-mule teams driven up and went into camp on the opposite side of the stream. I remarked to Pard that we were in luck and to saddle up and mount. He did so and we rode about a quarter of a mile in the road that our command had passed on, then we turned to the left and went into woods about two hundred yards from the road and unsaddled, and turned our horses loose under Pard's protest, he claiming that we at least should tie our horses, so that if we did not succeed, we would still have our horses. I replied that if we did not, that we would make better time walking, and that was what I proposed doing if I found I was too cowardly to mount a government mule when they now had Yanks for owners. His next objection was that we would not be able to find our saddles, and I said: "Yet you propose to tie your horse where he will probably starve, if the place is not found." I, by this time, saw I had a weak subject and could not depend on his aid. When we got within seventy-five yards of the teams, we stopped for a few minutes to take observation. I could see from the small camp fire that all was clear and that the two drivers had turned in for the night, so I suggested to Pard that he go to the nearest team and get a mule, and that I would go to the fartherest. He weakened and said he could not take the risk. I then said: "If you will strictly obey instructions, I will mount you; but if you think you cannot, return to your horse, and saddle and ride on." He agreed, so I told him to remain at the point he was then standing. I was soon examining the first team. It was at the front of the wagon, and did not take kindly to me and made some noise;

and there was soon a head and shoulder seen in front under wagon cover. I was looking for the driver to be aroused so I stayed squatted between the mules until he drew back, and then I continued my examination for a good mount; and as I had my idea set on a mare mule, I was delayed sometime in finding one and feeling of her limbs to see if she was sound. When I had made my choice, I soon made friends and very quietly unhitched and led off. I soon found my man and handed him the halter and told him to rub the mule's head and pet, to keep it from braying. I returned and unhitched another and it was contrary and made a noise but I had time to squat and pass under, unobserved, by each teamster looking out and why they did not miss the mule that I had taken was a mystery. They were soon back and quiet, as I went to the side of each wagon and from their breathing they were asleep. By this time the mules had somewhat familiarized my presence. I was soon out with Pard and handed him the halter that I held, and said: "You have my mule." Pard's mule brayed once while we were leading them away, but the boys were not disturbed of their rest. We were soon at our saddles, but saw nothing of our former saddle horses and I said to Pard I was more courteous to my horse than he, for I had patted him and said good bye and wished he would fall into the hands of a better master.

We were soon mounted; overtook our command while they were breakfasting the next morning. My mule was all one could ask for; gentle and a fine saddler and carried the C. S. brand. Pard's mule was good, but a poor saddler. We were soon through with breakfast and on the march. We passed through a small town and were halted some time. The officer was onto his job and had Pard and I ride at the head of the column and the boys in the rear posted. While we were halted, a runner came to the front and said we were followed by two men. Then Lieutenant Littlefield ordered us to hide behind the court house and when our pursuers passed on, for us to take a parallel road to the right. The squad was soon moving and all of the boys had caught on. The pursuers whipped by, bareheaded and without saddles, and were unmercifully guyed as they passed. They maintained a sweeping lope as long as I sighted them, and seemed intent on overtaking what they would have termed thieves, although they had no arms. We took a parallel road, as directed, for a few miles, then we returned to the main road. Pard protested and asked what we would do if our pursuers met us on the return. I said: "You saw that they had no arms; so, neither would be hurt, and I believe I would like to meet the boys anyhow and try and repay them for their honest effort to regain the mules, which I would do by telling them the war was over and to hitch up and drive as straight for home as they could, but to keep a close watch for, if they didn't, they would wake up some morning with the balance gone."

We saw no more of them and were soon with our command. Our number was decreasing daily by the men dropping out to visit relatives or friends, and I think that by the time we were a short way in Alabama, Fox Trammel, John Pipkin and I were the only ones of the original party who were holding to our westerly course. So we journeyed on as a party of three, found as a general thing, plenty for man and beast, and especially in Mississippi; and I think I saw more corn housed in one section of that state than I saw on my whole travels. We took advantage of this plentifulness of corn and moved but a few miles per day, feeding and resting our horses. We usually stopped early of an evening and would get our bread baked at some near by house, leaving one of the party as camp-keeper.

One evening, while we were in Alabama—it was Trammel's time to stay in camp—we were stopping a few hundred yards out from what looked to be a small village. John and I had taken our meal and were going to the first house to get bread baked. We saw quite a number of tenement houses built in two rows and facing each other, with a wide street between. We learned that it was the quarters for laborers for some iron industry, and from what I have learned since, it must have been near Sheffield. On entering the yard we saw quite a number of large, long poor rats and an old dog lying down. The rats seemed to have no fear of the dog and but little for John and me. Our curiosity was excited. When we went to the house, we found a mother, two daughters and a ten or twelve year old boy. We asked if we could get bread baked and they readily agreed. Our next query was: Why that dog did not kill the rats we saw running over and near him, and how came there to be so many. Their explanation was, that the Confederates had been for quite a while gathering commissary supplies and storing in the company's house and shop, and that there had been a great amount of corn handled through them and the rats had multiplied to such an extent that there were thousands of them burrowed in and about the storage rooms; that a short time since the Yankees had raided the place and burned all, but had let the people near by get out a lot before firing the buildings and that they had gotten out corn enough to bread them for some time, but the rats, from all appearances, to a large extent, escaped burning and had left the burned district and scattered among the near settlers and it looked as though they would devour all the food supply. That there was a good supply of chickens among the people and that the rats had eaten all but one old cock—that he had, from some cause, roosted well up in a tall tree and as yet they had not been able to get him, and that the occupants of the house next to them had a sow with six pigs a few weeks old, and that they had all been eaten. I had read of rat stories, and thought they were all highly colored; but from the number of rats I saw about the place and their starving appearance, I credited the statement. They said the dog killed rats by the dozens when they made their first appearance, but had apparently given up in disgust and would notice them only while eating. The house was a double pen log house with entry between. They used one room to stow their corn, which they had in boxes and barrels and some in sacks hung by cord to joist; and they had found no way to keep the rats from eating it and had already lost about half of their supply—said they made it their daily business to stop all holes that were gnawed through during the night and that they had used all devices that they could think or had heard of to destroy them; but were now nearly ready to give up, as they had no iron vessels to put corn in. John and I gave the outside of a room a thorough inspection; found quite a number of holes that had been stopped and a great number of places that were almost gnawed through. To the reader it may appear that the saving of about one dozen bushels of corn against rats would be a simple matter, but from my viewpoint it was not.

We received our bread and were invited to return after supper and they would show us the most practical way that they used to destroy the rats. But with the great amount that they had killed, and their neighbors doing likewise, with no perceptible lessening, the only remedy was starvation, as it looked to be a hopeless undertaking to kill them.

John and I returned about dark and from what we could see and the noise we heard, we concluded that a large percentage had not been reckoned by us from daylight observation. On our way to the house, John and I settled our claims to the young ladies—the older was mine and the younger, John's; so when we reached the house, each showed his favorite a choice and the young ladies proved to be nice, mannerly and sociable. This we did not learn on our breadbaking trip, as the mother did the talking for the crowd and the theme of conversation was rats, rats, and what was to become of her and family. After we had pleasantly conversed for a short time, we reminded the young ladies of their promise; for John and I seemed to be in the mother's condition, and, as it were, had rats on the brain. The boy was instructed to unstop a certain hole in entry, which gave the rats free access to the room and to get the sack, which looked to be a corn sack of usual size. The rats were watching the boy, I guess, for they seemed to commence entering the room at once, and from the squeaking and noise, John and I got excited at once, as we were sure there was a sack full of them in the room. The girls demurred, but John and I insisted— so John and his girl held the mouth of the sack over the hole, and my girl, the boy and I took a light and entered the room. The rats were not cowed by our entrance and several times I jumped backward to keep a grinning rat on a barrel or box from jumping on me, if such was his intention, for they surely made me think such was their aim. We ran a small amount in the sack, but there was quite a lot that would not return through the hole. So, after chasing and thumping for a while, we went out and were told if we had listened to them, we would have caught more rats, as killing rats in a room was not the game. We made no attempt to do so. The chimney hearth was of stone, and I took the sack as instructed and swung it up and gave the contents a few hard blows on the hearth and then emptied; and found thirteen dead rats. The girls pleasantly reminded us that "Men do not know everything," and if we had taken their advice and waited a few minutes longer, we would have gotten a sack full; and that without chasing a few straggling rats that did not want to go out. John and I promised to be good, and were. The hole was left open and by the time we had the rats killed and counted, there seemed to be all that was needed; but as John and I had promised the girls to let them call time, we kept mum. So we waited several minutes and as the rats were on my brain, I felt restless, but the girls were more used to the fun and seemed to enjoy the conversation, I thought to extremes, when there were rats to bag. Time was called and my girl and I took the sack, and after she had instructed me how to spread and hold the mouth of the sack, and said "All ready" John, his girl and the boy entered the room. I could hear John now and then, and he acted as though he was scared, but I knew he would come out with all honors, as I did; for the presence of his girl would hold him to his job. The rats commenced pouring into the sack as fast as they could singly pass through the hole. It was soon crowded to overflowing and my girl had not called time—a rat crowded out and was making fast flight up her clothes. She was up and dancing all kinds of steps. She finally got rid of the rat and quieted down. I could not enjoy the fun of the woman and the rat to any great extent for when she took her hands from the side of the sack, the rats commenced pouring out and I grabbed my side and stood up and then began shaking to settle what I could to the bottom, so I could close the mouth of the sack without getting bit. The rats were killed in the same manner as at first. When counted, there were twenty-three; so from the bulk killed there were at least as many escaped, for they had crowded in until the sack was full. I asked the young lady why she did not order closing the sack before it got so full, and she said that they were running in so fast that she got excited. I said we were now even, as I knew better; but I had agreed to be good and had done so; but I learned that women were somewhat as they had said of men: "That they did not know it all." We were soon in camp and comfortably stowed for the night.

After entering Mississippi, we concluded to head for Natchez and make our way across Mississippi River near that point, dodging the Yanks so as to keep our horses. We had no idea, as yet, as to how we would be treated by them. Early one day, when we were twenty odd miles from Natchez, we were overtaken by an elderly lady and son yet in his teens. They were in a light wagon behind a good team. They passed us and I said to the boys, "Let's ride up and see if we can't get the desired information." They demurred on the ground that they might be spies; but I said, have no fear for I take them to have been once wealthy natives, and if I was correct that they had no love for the Yankees. They agreed to ride up and let me do the talking. I was soon riding by the side of the wagon and Fox and John near behind. I proceeded without fear, and soon was well posted. She said she was the mother of the boy and was once wealthy and that their mission to the country was to try and get some chickens and eggs and had nearly made a failure; that she was a widow and was living with one of her sons-in-law, who lived several miles out from Natchez. That the old family home was only a short distance out from the city and was in charge of an old trusty negro man and woman, and her son stayed there part of the time, but there was but little doing as they had nothing but farm and implements left. She was thoroughly businesslike and asked me if I would sell the mule, as the war being over, she would make an effort to restock her farm. I told her I would like to sell, provided the other two did, but could not if our stock was not sold as a whole, as we had agreed on striking Texas before parting, and if we were so unfortunate as to be dismounted, we would walk. She said she would give me one hundred dollars in greenbacks for the mule. My reply was: "What for the two horses?" She said, "It is farm mules I want." I said: "The horses are young, able-bodied; fine saddlers, and one of them was among the speedy horses of the Texas Rangers and would either plow or trade to advantage, and if she struck a sport that the bay, or Trammel's horse, would bring her a fine pair of mules, and that she need have no fear of letting the proposed purchaser test its speed qualities, and if she made a fair offer on the horses, I would accept the price offered for the mule." She then offered for Trammel's horse, the same as for the mule, and said for Pipkin's horse she would sell him to her son who lived a short distance ahead for eighty dollars gold, which was about equal in price to the others. My reply was: "I will see what the boys say and am in hopes they will accept, for under the conditions, your price is liberal, but we could get more by selling in Texas, especially for Trammel's horse, as he was inclined on the sporting side of life and knew that his horse had good value as a racer." Pipkin and Trammel had dropped some distance behind and had beckoned me several times, but I did not heed call until the woman and I were understood. I told her that my mule was in the same condition as all first class mules of the South, with C.S. or U.S. branded on them and that mine was C.S. She said she did not think the Yankees would bother. I dropped back and the boys seemed worried at me and said that we had better shake the old woman at once as we would soon be within the Yankee lines if we followed her; and that she would then give us away and we would be dismounted and probably detained. I told them that the woman was what she had claimed to be and to take my judgment for that. They started by pronouncing her a spy and I started to prove my first impression correct and that I had found it so in every particular; she only wanted my mule and had no fear of the C.S. brand. I said: "Boys, I guess that looks funny to you, as you have been guying me for a time about not being able to sell mule, and here I am, with mule the leader in a sale: so do as you please, and I will do the same; but you will have lost the chance of a sale if the mule is not a consideration now. Let's ride up and overtake her and talk to her before I accept as individual." So we were soon with the wagon, and she said: "See that house ahead? That is my son's place; if you young men wish to sell, say so, as that horse would belong to him (pointing to John's) and I want to pay for him." John agreed and in less than fifteen minutes had eighty dollars in gold pocketed. She told her son to send to a place of delivery the other two horses and get his. We then rode on a few miles and stopped at her son-in-law's. We were met at the front porch and had our clothes well dusted. I did not tell it, but I knew it was the first time I ever had the other fellow to do my dusting, and as the other boys acted like they had been raised to such usage, I guess they were in about the same plight as I; but I have since thought that we did not fool the negro servant, as we did not tip him, which was evidence that we were of the "poor white trash," or what the slaves of the well-to-do called the "poor white bucker."* I don't know when, where, nor how the word "bucker" originated; but well knew its meaning, and that was, that a rich man's slave was better than a poor white man and was often used as a slur by a negro owned by the rich to one owned by poor white people. We were asked in and seated in a finely furnished parlor. I don't think that the old lady sat down until she had paid us, as agreed, and stated that Trammel and I turn our mounts in at a farm near town and her son would go down with the wagon, and John. We soon had a nice dinner, then returned to the parlor and enjoyed music for a time. Then we started for the farm and were soon among outing Yankees, picking berries. I was fearful they would see the C.S. on the mule and as I had a large leather pouch or haversack, I put the strop on the pommel of the saddle and let the pouch cover the brand. My fear was soon allayed as our passing did not seem to attract their attention. We soon were at the farm house and the old colored man took charge of our stock, and the old colored woman had a good supper prepared at the proper time. The young man sent to town and got an ample supply of whiskey for an all night's carousal. He seemed to be in the height of his glory and said he felt honored to have the privilege of entertaining us and for us to eat, drink and be merry—and we surely did until about 2 A.M. None of us drank to get drunk, but the past and future was no part of our rejoicing—it was the pres-

---

* The word *buckra* was used by black people in Africa to denote a white man. The term came to America with the captured slaves and the pronunciation seems to have been altered slightly.

ent, and we sure made each minute count. We hugged, danced, sang and halloaed to our soul's content and our young friend joined in. All our monkey acts would end up in a great ha-ha laugh. We got a few hours' sleep and were called for breakfast. The old colored man had a rig geared up and the mule was one of the team. I asked the old man if he was not afraid to drive mule into town, and he said: "I have brand to the tongue side," and when he struck the city he would drive fast, which he did, and when we alighted at the hotel, he drove away fast; and I guess he got back all O.K. —he told me he would soon have the brand blurred or ironed out, as he called it. We were soon in a hotel and registered. From there we reported at headquarters, were paroled and given transportation. Pipkin and Trammel went via New Orleans, I to Alexandria, Louisiana. I changed boats at mouth of Red River. All seemed to be "busted" on the boat but we three; and we did the charity act by making quite a lot of the old boys forget their cares for a time. I walked from Alexandria to my sister's, a Mrs. Allen, which was forty miles out, in the direction of my home. I stayed there about one month and had an enjoyable time. My brother-in-law came to Texas with me; we drove through in a two-horse buggy. I left sister's with a twenty dollar greenback bill and got accommodations to Sabine River free, as no one would take it—for the want of confidence or lack of money of like kind; all seemed to be afraid of greenbacks.

I was told by several before leaving sister's that the Texans were accused of a good deal of horse stealing during the war, from Louisiana, and I would do the wrong thing in traveling by claiming to be a Texan. I asked if none were taken by Louisiana thieves and run into other states and sold. Their reply was: "Texans were accused of it," so I again thought of the old saying, "Give a dog a bad name and you had as well kill it."

Allen and I called at a widow's house late one evening, to stay all night. It was near Lake Charles, and if I remember correctly, it was in or near the section that is called "Big Woods." Her son was a member of Company "F," 5th Texas Infantry, and was a fine young fellow, and he and I were quite chummy. He seemed to think a great deal of his mother and sisters, and often spoke of them; and would hand me letters from home to read—and from their tone, their love for each other was mutual. He had often told me to be sure and call on them if I ever passed that way, so in time's onward flight, I received from his dying lips his last message on this earth to the mother and sisters, and I promised to deliver it, if in my power to do so. When I entered the yard, the mother and two sisters, as I took them to be, were sitting on the front gallery. I advanced to the steps, and spoke—asked to stay all night. The old lady seemed to be terribly out of sorts, for her reply was: "No," and a shower of words that came so thick and fast that I could get no chance to explain, so I stood and listened as long as my nature would permit; turned, went to the buggy and drove some distance and stopped for the night. Allen asked if I was not going to deliver the message. I said, "no, how could I: for her words were not of the soothing kind, and she would not give me a chance to speak; and that I had long since tired of war tales of woe and abuse and I guessed I had done wrong, but my nature was such that my passion had overbalanced reason." Allen stopped at the place, on his return home and delivered the message, so the mother and sisters learned about the young man's ending.

When we arrived at the Sabine River near Niblets Bluff,

there was a long ferriage as the river was up. The ferryman changed without hesitancy my twenty dollar bill. I knew nothing of the difference in value between U.S. currency and specie, so he made the change to suit his own ideas and I received mostly gold which I found upon arriving in Beaumont to be at a premium rate sufficient to purchase a greater amount than twenty dollars in green backs, so as it were, the ferryman had paid to cross us over the river. I think of this incident every time I read of some fellow returning amounts to the conscience fund, but as yet have never divied up. We left the team on the east side of Neches river and crossed on the T. & N. O. R. R.* trestle, which was under water.

In Beaumont I found my old father and two small half-sisters.† My brother and stepmother had both died of yellow fever and a young half-brother had gone to other parts and had joined the sporting element as a race horse rider. I found John Pipkin's‡ old father, who was once a well to do farmer, following two or three worn teams, doing the draying for the people through Beaumont's mud, and preaching of a Sunday to the natives. He preached for the good, and not for the gold; as he was of the old-time sort, and tried to make one feel better after talking than before; was a pleasant and fluent talker and lived on the bright side of life; performed marriage

---

* A History of Jefferson County, Texas: From Wilderness to Reconstruction, by W. T. Block, shows that the Texas and New Orleans Railroad was constructed in 1860 and 1861. It ran from Houston to Orange, Texas.
† Thomas Fletcher married Margaret Mouchet, of St. Landry Parish, Louisiana, in 1849, after the death of Bill's mother. Their children were Henry (named for the uncle who had turned Bill away), Beatrice Vandalia, and Alzenia.
‡ Pastor John Fletcher Pipkin was Beaumont's earliest resident minister. Bill admired him because he ministered to everyone regardless of their religious affiliation.

ceremonies of soldier boys, when called upon, and would accept nothing: but would say, "You boys have merited all you will ever get, and I feel it an honored privilege to have the opportunity to join in marriage, such men."

John and I enjoyed our return to the full extent, I guess —as well, or better, than the boys of today would, returning under similar service to the present or improved Beaumont. John and I, before enlisting to full citizenship, or going to work, as it were, were giving but little thought of tomorrow, and were after a good time; and each of us had seen service enough to learn not to pine over the by-gone or carry hatred for a victorious foe. Our company, at times, caused considerable comment. There was at that time a company of soldiers stationed at Beaumont, and John and I were soon acquainted with a lot of the boys; found them to be nice, jovial young fellows, if they were born North of Mason and Dixon's line. The boys were well equipped with cash, and liberal. John and I, after going through with a four years' experience, had learned something about individuality, so, if it did not hurt our pride to take a drink with the Yanks, we had committed no crime, and it was none of the other fellow's business. I was spoken to, upon several occasions, about John's and my friendship for the Yanks, and the surprise it was causing— coming from two young men who had borne their part so well during the struggle. My reply would be: "The war is over and I am following the North Carolinian's advice" (Telling the story).

When Allen started to return home, I gave him what cash I had left to make the trip on—then I was "busted" and ready for work, so I made application for work at the Long & Carroll Sawmill. I had worked at the mill at different times before the war—my last wages were $35.00 per month and board. Long told me when I started to war, that if I came out whole, he wanted me to come to the mill and learn to handle it. I promised to do so. When I told him I was ready for work, and if there was an opening, I would appreciate it, he said: "All right, Bill, and I will pay you one dollar per month greater than the other laborers;" that he was paying fifteen dollars, but would give me sixteen. I declined, saying: "Four years lost and wages cut."

So I went home and gathered up father's old carpenter tools and went on a job at $1.50 per day, about one hundred feet from the place where I left off work.

FINIS.

AFTERWORD

by Vallie Fletcher Taylor

"He was a man before his time." "He was a true visionary." I heard such statements about my great-grandfather frequently when I was a child. How, I wondered, could a man be before his time? Later, as I lived through the 1960s, I realized that Bill Fletcher's beliefs would have been far more suited to that era of dynamic social change than they were for the conservative society in which he lived a century before.

William "Bill" Andrew Fletcher died many years before my birth. However, his stories, philosophy, humor, and compassion were passed on to me by two people who had been very close to him. My father, his namesake, and my great-aunt Vallie, his only daughter, were the wisdom keepers for our family. Great-grandfather was a legend in East Texas, so they were anxious for me to know the truth about the influences that shaped his life.

Vallie Fletcher never married. Instead, she devoted her life to her work as an artist and to keeping her father's memory alive. The varied hues and rhythms of her landscapes enlivened the walls of our home when I was young. To me, though, her most valuable work was the portrait of her father that she so skillfully painted on the canvas of my imagination.

Bill Fletcher grew up on the edge of the dense forests of western Louisiana and eastern Texas in the 1840s and 1850s. His formal schooling was minimal, but enough to allow him to become an avid reader, especially in the fields of science and mechanics. From the time he was a very young boy, the teachers who served him best were those who he encountered on his many lone trips into the woodlands to hunt, fish, or simply enjoy the natural beauty of his surroundings.

In those days, East Texas was a new frontier for migrants from the South seeking land that was either cheap or free. The forests became a safe haven for people who, for their own reasons, were escaping any type of settlement and creating their own solitary existence. So Bill, the son of an overseer, carpenter, and slave runner, encountered many a runaway slave. He shared his wild game with them and, if they seemed willing to communicate, he would linger and visit. From these chance meetings he learned sensitivity to the needs and feelings of others and uncritical acceptance of other races.

At times Indians befriended the young hunter and taught him wilderness skills that would serve him well during years to come. He was an eager student and enjoyed the process of sharpening his five senses as he developed his intuition within his wooded surroundings. The Indian belief that there is one Great Spirit that dwells in all living things was one that he chose to adopt and live by. This awareness made him unreceptive to organized religious groups for the remainder of his life.

Bill grew into a wilderness pioneer, self-sufficient and physically hardened. His father, Thomas Fletcher, taught him carpentry, to love history and literature, and to distrust preachers and politicians. Though his parents had left behind their homes in South Carolina and Tennessee for a rough and rustic frontier life, they both instructed him in the manners expected of a southern gentleman.

The outdoor existence Bill enjoyed in his childhood helped him meet the challenges of a life in which he would be both a rich man and a poor man. During the Civil War, he added the roles of beggarman and thief. This book relates his wartime experiences in the infantry as a part of Hood's Texas Brigade and in the fearless cavalry unit known as Terry's Texas Rangers.

After the Confederate defeat, Bill returned to East Texas and took up his father's carpenter tools to lay the foundation for a career in the lumber business. In 1865, he went to work at Long and Co. Lumber Mill and used his salary to buy stock in the company. The company's president was James Long, who had three sisters. Bill fell in love with one sister, Julian, and married her later that year. Julian came from a family that could trace its roots back to Virginia landowners in 1591. She was polished, educated, and a pillar of the Southern Baptist Church. Despite their differences the marriage between the proper southern lady and the rough-hewn millworker was a happy one. They eventually became parents of four sons and a daughter.

When James Long died in 1873, Bill became president of the company, renamed it Long Manufacturing Company, and converted it to a shingle mill. He also owned Village Mills Lumber Company and the Texas Tram and Lumber Company. With three brothers-in-law, he formed an interlocking directorate that began buying up large acreages of East Texas timberlands and acquiring more mills in Texas and Louisiana.

Bill has been given credit for developing the export market for yellow pine, and one newspaper article stated that the nation's first load of lumber to be exported went from his Texas Tram and Lumber Co., via schooner, to Cuba. Journalists chronicled Bill's rapid rise and financial success in lumbering's golden era, and as he became more affluent, they even promoted him in rank. Lumber trade journals ran articles about "the patents and inventions of Captain W. A. Fletcher." Later, this was raised to Colonel Fletcher. The Rebel private found these fictitious promotions amusing.

The Standard Blue Book of Texas, 1908 edition, states, "W. A. Fletcher, the most distinguished living lumber man today . . . was a practical saw mill operator, being considered the most skillful mechanic and competent millwright in Texas. It was in a great measure due to his thorough knowledge of the mill business that the companies he was connected with were conducted so successfully."

In *Emerald of the Neches*, historian W. T. Block observes that few Texans were aware of the national stature of W. A. Fletcher, who "was both inventive and a business genius." Block quotes an old copy of *The Lumberman* that called Bill "The Old Man Eloquent." He was asked to make a speech about the Fletcher Gauge for scaling lumber, while representing Texas at a lumbermen's convention in Chicago. Bill declined the honor, but, "The way he dealt in the hundreds of an inch [while explaining to a gauge committee] was enough to make one's head swim."

Historian and archivist Jonathan Gerland writes:

> William A. Fletcher was an integral part of the enterprising spirit which revitalized Texas following the Civil War and Reconstruction. By successfully utilizing natural resources at

hand, he made an indelible mark in the forests and sawdust of East Texas. His hard work and determination culminated in the construction and operation of sawmills and railroads in a vast, but sparsely populated area, providing jobs and community services for hundreds of families.

When eastern and northern industrial designs did not suit his needs, Fletcher designed and built his own machinery, including massive combination steam log loaders and log skidders which were compatible with his logging railroads. As a patriot, industrialist, businessman, philanthropist, and mechanical inventor, W. A. Fletcher is a fitting symbol of East Texas' golden era of prosperity and industrialization.

In January 1895, the *Galveston Daily News* reported that the Texas Tram and Lumber Company had smashed a world's record for one day's cut of long-leaf yellow pine. This cut was done with one huge circular saw that Bill had designed and built.

Though Bill Fletcher's reputation grew in prominence, he remained a relatively shy man. Rather than accept the many invitations he was extended to give talks at national conventions, he wrote the book *Something New in Logging* in 1896. This small book explained the operation of his (then) revolutionary new invention, the Fletcher Log Hauling and Loading Machine. Bill became excited by and enjoyed using the unique inventions of others. Shortly after Alexander Graham Bell's invention, the first phone line in East Texas was stretched between two of his lumber mills. His friends and associates frequently urged him to run for public office or to join some social or fraternal organization. He would laugh at the idea and declined all offers in favor of a private life totally devoted to his family.

Since the aftermath of the Battle of Chickamauga, Bill had nurtured a special debt of gratitude to the Catholic Sisters of Charity. He was sure that the care given him by these compassionate women in Augusta, Georgia, had saved his leg from amputation. Though his numerous philanthropies were a matter of public record, he had always hoped to do something special to honor this order. So in 1897, Bill began working with the mother house, St. Mary's Infirmary in Galveston, to plan a hospital for Beaumont. He secured land on the Neches River and donated funds and lumber to build their hospital, which would be called Hotel Dieu.

For his continuing contributions to the sisters, he received a great deal of criticism from Protestant pulpits in East Texas. His daughter later wrote, "He believed in a Supreme Being, but he did not understand many ministers who preached in that day. He was made to feel embarrassed and self-conscious by their personal remarks alluding to an influential man who did much harm in what they called his influence against Christianity." People who did not understand his spiritual beliefs, including some of his in-laws, assumed that he was an atheist.

My father remembered the many Sunday dinners that became cold while one of their pious relatives gave a sermon-length blessing. He often laughed at the memory of his grandfather surprising the assembled family by offering to return thanks. Bill shocked the adults and delighted the hungry children by reciting, "Bless the meat and darn the skin. Back your ears and all pitch in. Amen."

From the time my father was a toddler, Bill devised all sorts of ingenious schemes to extricate young Bill from his mother's prim Victorian parlor and unyielding set of rules of proper behavior. He often resorted to morning visits in which he would simply kidnap his grandson for the day. The two Bills would appear on horseback by sunset, having spent their time together out of doors.

Bill Senior's dislike for pretentiousness, which he often expressed, was balanced by an acute sensitivity to the needs of others. "My father reminded me in his hospitality of the priest in *Les Misérables*," wrote his daughter. "Everyone passing his home was welcome to come in. Both white and Negro came to him for advice and help, and he never failed to respond generously."

Retirement was not what Bill Fletcher had in mind when he sold his lumber mills in 1902. He purchased 2,658 acres on the Orange County side of the Neches River, built a country home, and named it Park Farm. There he grew experimental food crops and raised horses, cattle, sheep, and chickens. To the delight of his grandchildren, he invented and built an assortment of mechanical rides, creating a family amusement center.

There was always a copy of the *Scientific American* on Bill's bedside table, but for relaxation he chose detective stories. With more free time, he took the opportunity to create a written record of his Civil War experiences. His plan was to write a book and print enough copies to give family and friends and to the Old Soldiers' Home in Austin. Vallie Fletcher wrote, "He would read what he had written during the day . . . as we sat in the evening before the big open fireplace in my mother's bedroom."

Rebel Private: Front and Rear was published in 1908. Some copies were given to old acquaintances, and the rest were stored in the family home in Beaumont. No thought was ever given to the historical value of "Grandpa's book." Unfortunately, this large Victorian home caught fire, and a portion of it, along with almost all of the neatly stacked books, burned. The copies that were saved were smoke- or water-damaged.

At some point, a copy of *Rebel Private* found its way into the Library of Congress Rare Book Room, where historians converged upon it. In the 1940s, Aunt Vallie received letters and visits from many of these people. I remember her reading me a letter from "a nice lady named Margaret Mitchell." Mitchell wrote that *Rebel Private: Front and Rear* had been her single most valuable research tool when writing *Gone With the Wind.*

Bill Fletcher died of pneumonia at Park Farm on January 4, 1915. His body was put on a launch and, accompanied by friends and family members, he took his last ride down the Neches River back to Beaumont. A simple service was held at the family home on Calder Avenue with his friend, attorney R. A. Greer, officiating.

The schools, banks, two district courts, the county court, stores, and businesses all closed out of respect on the day of his funeral. The *Beaumont Enterprise* wrote, "It is doubtful if the funeral of any other citizen of Beaumont ever attracted such widespread interest in this city or was marked by more general recognition." A large number of black people attended the services, which was unheard of in the strictly segregated East Texas environment of 1915.

Greer ended the eulogy with these words:

He was a believer in temperance in all things, but despised law-made morals. His conscience was his guide; he believed in a Supreme Power but denied the right of any man, set of men, creed or doctrine to dictate to him his moral code.

He believed every man was the keeper of his own conscience and was alone responsible for his life. He believed that heaven and hell were both present on this earth, and whether you were happy or unhappy was according to the life you led.

He was not afraid to die because he had led the life that deserved no punishment. He was a patriot without personal ambition. He needs no monument erected to him by us, for his life is indelibly engraved on the tablets of his country.

Beaumont, Texas, October 1994

· A NOTE ON THE TYPE ·

The typeface used in this book is one of many versions of
Garamond, a modern homage to—rather than, strictly speaking, a revival of—the celebrated fonts of Claude Garamond
(c.1480–1561), the first founder to produce type on a large
scale. Garamond's type was inspired by Francesco Griffo's De
Ætna type (cut in the 1490s for Venetian printer Aldus Ma-
nutius and revived in the 1920s as Bembo), but its letter
forms were cleaner and the fit between pieces of type improved. It therefore gave text a more harmonious overall appearance than its predecessors had, becoming the basis of all
romans created on the Continent for the next two hundred
years; it was itself still in use through the eighteenth century.
Besides the many "Garamonds" in use today, other typefaces
derived from his fonts are Granjon and Sabon (despite their
being named after other printers).